Competing to Be Really, REALLY Good

The behind-the-scenes drama of capability-building competition in the automobile industry

The LTCB International Library Trust

The LTCB (Long-Term Credit Bank of Japan) International Library Trust, established in July 2000, is the successor to the LTCB International Library Foundation. It carries on the mission that the foundation's founders articulated as follows:

> The world is moving steadily toward a borderless economy and deepening international interdependence. Amid economic globalization, Japan is developing ever-closer ties with nations worldwide through trade, through investment, and through manufacturing and other localized business operations.
>
> Japan's global activity is drawing attention to its political, economic, and social systems and to the concepts and values that underlie those systems. But the supply of translations of Japanese books about those and other Japan-related subjects has not kept pace with demand.
>
> The shortage of foreign-language translations of Japanese books about Japanese subjects is attributable largely to the high cost of translating and publishing. To address that issue, the LTCB International Library Foundation funds the translation and the distribution of selected Japanese works about Japan's politics, economy, society, and culture.

International House of Japan, Inc., manages the publishing activities of the LTCB International Library Trust, and Chuo Mitsui Trust and Banking Company, Ltd., manages the trust's financial assets.

LTCB International Library Trust/International House of Japan

Competing to Be Really, REALLY Good

The behind-the-scenes drama of capability-building competition in the automobile industry

Takahiro Fujimoto
Executive Director
Manufacturing Management Research Center
University of Tokyo

Translated by **Brian Miller**

This book was originally published in 2003 in a somewhat different form by Chuokoron-Shinsha, Inc., as *Noryoku Kochiku Kyoso: Nihon no Jidosha Sangyo wa Naze Tsuyoi no ka*. International House of Japan retains the English-language translation rights under contract with Takahiro Fujimoto and through the courtesy of Chuokoron-Shinsha.

First English edition published March 2007 by International House of Japan
11-16, Roppongi 5-chome, Minato-ku, Tokyo 106-0032, Japan
Tel: +81-3-3470-9059   Fax: +81-3-3470-3170
E-mail: ihj@i-house.or.jp

Printed in Japan
ISBN 978-4-924971-21-9

Contents

Author's Introduction to the English Edition

This book originally appeared in Japanese in 2003 as *Noryoku Kochiku Kyoso* (Capability-Building Competition; Chuokoron-Shinsha). For more than 20 years, I had conducted empirical research on the world automobile industry as a researcher in the fields of technology and operations management. I had the good fortune to participate in trailblazing surveys of international competitiveness in the automobile industry at Harvard University in the late 1980s while doing my doctoral work under Professor Kim Clark and as a member since the mid-1980s of the Massachusetts Institute of Technology–based International Motor Vehicle Program. My participation in those surveys followed related work at Mitsubishi Research Institute in the early 1980s and preceded my present work as head of the Manufacturing Management Research Center at the University of Tokyo.

I wrote this book during a period of financial hardship for the Japanese automobile industry. Japan's automakers were struggling with the stubborn economic stagnation that followed the collapse of the nation's bubble economy of the 1980s. I had described my previous research findings in several publications, including the books *Product Development Performance* (with Kim Clark, 1991) and *The Evolution of a Manufacturing System at Toyota* (1999). Those findings had confirmed repeatedly that, on average, Japanese factories and technical centers in the automotive sector consistently led the world in assembly productivity, manufacturing quality, development lead time, and development efficiency. I had taken an interest in the contrast between the consistency of Japanese automakers in key indicators of manufacturing performance and the fluctuating perceptions of their strengths. That contrast had convinced me of the need for distinguishing between financial performance and basic manufacturing performance in evaluating automakers.

Capability-building competition

Throughout the history of the automobile industry, companies' financial results have swung sharply in reflection of temporal factors, such as business cycles, currency exchange rates, energy prices, and managerial mistakes. Fundamental capability and performance in the manufacturing (*monozukuri*) workplace (*genba*) have developed far more gradually and steadily. I have sought in this book to sketch a dynamic industry analysis based on direct observation of the manufacturing workplace. Organizational capability in *monozukuri* arises through evolutionary processes, which is the reason for the slow pace of change in *genba* performance. And driving the evolution of those processes is *capability-building competition*—rivalry among manufacturing workplaces in pursuing better sets of organizational routines.

This book identifies capability-building competition as the main engine of industrial development. Media coverage of competition in the automobile industry has tended to dwell on eye-catching stories, such as trade disputes and mergers and acquisitions. Those stories, however, are but a sideshow, at most, in the larger tale of competition among automakers. Companies' viability ultimately depends on their initiative in capability building. Never in the long and lamentable history of trade wars have protectionist measures succeeded in keeping companies viable that shirked that responsibility. Nor have manufacturers been notably successful in strengthening their long-term viability through acquisitions or alliances aimed simply at increasing economies of scale. Only where the partners have provided carefully for promoting mutual capability learning have tie-ups proved consistently beneficial.

I explore in this book the relationship between manufacturing capability and product architecture. The chief criterion I use for product architecture is the dichotomy of integral architecture, where the components interact organically in complex ways, and modular architecture, where the components function semiautonomously and interact through simple interfaces. I demonstrate that Japanese manufacturers have accumulated capabilities especially well suited to products of integral architecture, such as passenger cars.

Manufacturers in the same nation, exposed to a similar competitive environment, tend to accumulate similar organizational capabilities. Japanese manufacturers in the latter half of the 20th century, for example, contended with chronic shortages of labor, cash, and materials even as they encountered huge growth opportunities. Their ever so rational response to those constraints included building stable, long-term relationships with suppliers and adopting long-term employment. Those practices produced a rich accumulation of capabilities—embodied quintessentially in the Toyota Production System—based on smooth coordination between assembly manufacturers and their parts suppliers and on good communication among employees. Reinforcing the manufacturers' coordination- and communication-based capabilities were related practices, such as multiskill training for employees, which engendered flexibility in allocating resources.

Coordination and communication are more important in products of integral architecture than in those of modular architecture, and the comparative advantage of Japanese manufacturers in integral-architecture products is readily evident in export performance. My statistical research findings reveal that the export ratio for Japanese products is higher among products of more-integral architecture.

Another important consideration in manufacturing competitiveness is the geographical placement of the design function. Traditional trade theory has placed heavy emphasis on comparative advantage. Production resources for integral-architecture products tend to coalesce, however, around the sites of design activity. "New trade theory" implicitly accounts for that tendency in its attribution of increasing returns to scale and product differentiation. That invites attention to the geography of design and to the reasons for that geography.

A lot of water has passed under the bridge since this book first appeared in Japanese in 2003. Automakers prone to dramatic fluctuations in business and financial performance have—well—undergone more fluctuations in business and financial performance. Equally significant, however, is the "boring" side of the industry: the automakers who remain unflaggingly profitable and who simply keep on growing.

Shifts in currency exchange rates might buffet automakers' price competitiveness in export markets. A phenomenally successful model might inflate an automaker's earnings for a year or two. But the automakers that keep chugging along through it all are those that focus less on such aspects of "surface competitiveness" than on the "deep competitiveness" essentials of training employees, minimizing inventories, improving quality, shortening lead time, and otherwise fortifying their organizational capability.

Building capabilities in manufacturing is a long-term challenge, and the basic emphases of the book published in 2003 remain as pertinent today as then. This book has previously appeared in Korean and Chinese, and I am delighted that it is now available to English-language readers. I am grateful for the conscientious treatment the book has received from Brian Miller, a translator well versed in Japanese manufacturing management, and from Yasuo Saji and his colleagues at the LTCB International Library and at its commercial imprint, I-House Press. Brian has reedited the text to focus on the content most relevant to Western readers, but the essential message of the original is here in full.

Tokyo
February 2007

Foreword

Discussion of the prodigious strengths asserted by Japan's automakers since the 1970s has tended to center on product quality and price competitiveness. The author endeavors in this book to describe the capability-building competition that has underlain those strengths.

Japan's automakers nurtured their world-beating strengths by striving tenaciously to outdo one another in building organizational capability in manufacturing. Capability-building competition has occurred in every nation and in every era, at least since the Industrial Revolution. It became especially intense, however, in the automotive sector and some other sectors of Japanese manufacturing in the postwar years. We will examine the reasons for that development on the following pages. We will also examine why capability building has been a notably decisive factor in competitiveness in the automobile industry—particularly in small passenger cars.

The automobile industry has been a uniquely robust and resilient sector of Japanese industry. Japan's automakers, led by Toyota, have been so strong for so long that their success might even seem a special case. Observers might dismiss that success as offering little in the way of relevant lessons for companies in other industries. That would be a mistake. The experience of Japan's automakers, including their mistakes, offers numerous lessons of tremendous value for companies in every industry. Everyone in manufacturing and in the service sector has much to learn from the capability building and from the competition in capability building that have unfolded in Japan's automobile industry. The present work is, in large part, an effort to highlight the broader lessons of that tale.

1 Competition in Capability Building

1. Overview

Some companies assert a persistent edge over competitors and post perennial gains in sales and earnings. Those corporate paragons typically possess valuable accumulations of proprietary knowledge and other important strategic resources. They also tend to exhibit excellence in organizational routine: employee behavior shaped by well-established rules and traditions. All of those strengths figure in organizational capability. We further define a successful company's organizational capability as being unique to the company, as being difficult for other companies to emulate, and as supporting continuing gains in competitiveness.

Companies can foster organizational capability in any phase of operations, including administrative functions, as well as R&D, manufacturing, and marketing. Japan's automakers owe their global preeminence largely to superior organizational capability in manufacturing and in closely related functions, such as R&D and purchasing. The author therefore focuses in this work on that facet of organizational capability.

Products as media and information

We need to recognize before proceeding that competitiveness in manufacturing is more than organizational capability and that even manufacturers of unexceptional organizational capability can be competitive. All too many proselytizers of organizational capability succumb to equating that capability tautologically with business success. That tendency is especially common among the resource-base theorists in the United States. To avoid churning tautologies, the author will endeavor to cite concrete examples of organizational capability in manufacturing. We will regard organizational capability as an information system, and we will seek examples of that capability in the unending exchange of product design information between companies and the marketplace.

1

FIGURE 1-1

Products as Amalgams of Information and Media

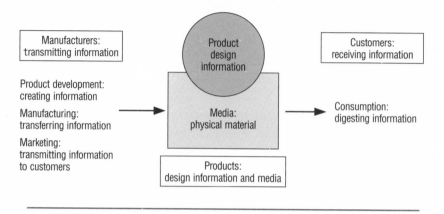

Goods and services are essentially materials—tangible and intangible media—infused with design information (fig. 1-1). Our first task, therefore, is to track the flow of design information: where the information arises, where it ferments, where it accumulates, and the path it takes en route to the final product. Mapping the creation and the transfer of information gives us a sketch of value-generating activity at providers of products and services.

The author, a university professor, is engaged in the education segment of the service sector. He provides students with knowledge and information through the barely tangible medium of vibrating air—lectures—and through the more-tangible medium of paper handouts. Similarly, automakers provide car buyers with, among other things, 0.8-millimeter-thick sheet metal infused with information about exterior design and body properties.

Professors and automakers alike infuse media with information and dispatch the resultant packages of information to customers. We can thus regard all business sectors as information industries. The information might be digital—as in the bits and bytes of the information technology industry—or it might be any kind of pattern used to represent product and service attributes. Information about product structure and function passes through computers, paper, plastic film, human brains, clay models, dies, and other media on its way into finished goods and services.

FIGURE 1-2

Production as the Transfer of Design Information

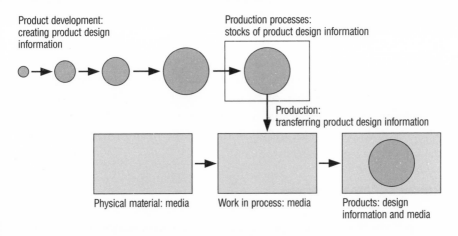

Product development:
creating product design
information

Production processes:
stocks of product design information

Production:
transferring product design information

Physical material: media   Work in process: media   Products: design
information and media

Production as the transfer of design information

Once we comprehend products as media infused with information, we can understand product development as the creation of design information and production as the transfer of that information to products. Companies' product development people create design information, and the companies then allocate that information among different production processes. The information flows into the media of materials and of work in process. That transfer of information into products is what we ordinarily refer to as production activity (fig. 1-2). And the way a company handles the flow of information among processes defines a big part of the company's identity.

Every manufactured item that we consume, be it a car, a personal computer, or whatever, is the product of that flow of information. Someone at the manufacturer designs the product, and the company purchases material—media—in accordance with the design information and transfers that information to the media. Manufacturing semiconductor devices, for example, centers on transferring design information optically through photomasks to silicon chips. Machining mechanical components, on the other hand, typically consists of transferring design information programmed in computerized machine tools and stored in the knowledge and skills of employees to raw metal. Stamping automobile bodies, meanwhile, is a matter of transferring information embedded in metal dies to sheet metal.

The design information, in combination with its medium, progresses from the production process through the marketing process to the marketplace. Customers there purchase the product, extract and consume the design information, and enjoy whatever benefits that it confers. The companies study the response of consumers and employ their findings in developing new products; that is, in generating new design information. That feedback completes the cycle of the flow of information between manufacturers and their customers.

Product competitiveness

We commonly regard competitiveness as the performance of companies and products relative to other companies and products in the marketplace. Competitiveness, in that sense, is the ability to survive at rivals' expense. We will focus in this work on that ability in manufacturing. To analyze the connection between organizational capability and corporate competitiveness, we need to examine the cause-and-effect sequence from (1) organizational capability through (2) the underlying, "deep" competitiveness of production processes and R&D to (3) the manifest, "surface" competitiveness of customer appeal.

The competitiveness of individual products is their effectiveness in satisfying customers and in attracting new purchasers. We sometimes discover short-term discrepancies between products' appeal to owners and their appeal to prospective owners. But lasting competitiveness for products depends on a sound combination of both kinds of appeal.

Some products, for example, exert superficial appeal that attracts droves of new customers but have fundamental flaws that ultimately leave the customers dissatisfied. Sooner or later, word of mouth from the dissatisfied customers reaches the audience of prospective customers, and the products lose their ability to attract new purchasers. Conversely, we can imagine products that owners love but that are superficially unappealing to prospective purchasers. The inability of those products to attract new purchasers, left unresolved, will marginalize the products in the marketplace.

Let us return to our characterization of products as media infused with design information. Product competitiveness becomes a matter of companies' success in providing customers with packages of information that is both initially persuasive and ultimately convincing.

Competitiveness from different standpoints

Product competitiveness from the vantage of the marketplace is a composite of the four P's: product (specifications, quality, and performance); price; promotion; and place (sales channel). Each P is a conduit for information that companies supply to customers. The four P's together constitute the surface competitiveness of products—the products' outward, overt appeal to customers.

From the vantage of the workplace, product competitiveness is a composite of quality, cost, and delivery. Those three elements, widely known as QCD, are standard measures of factory performance. The author supplements QCD with a fourth measure, flexibility (F), to support comprehensive evaluations of competitiveness in manufacturing.

Quality

In QCD&F, we construe quality to encompass every product-specific element that figures in customer satisfaction. Our definition of quality thus includes such elements as product performance, specifications, and styling, as well as the indicators of quality in the narrowest sense, such as basic functionality, durability, and dimensional accuracy. In automobiles, total product quality thus includes performance criteria, such as acceleration, maximum speed, and handling, along with comfort, appearance, and status value, as well as the basic elements of safety and reliability.

The two principal determinants of vehicle quality are design quality and manufacturing quality. Design quality is the level of performance and functionality expressed in the design drawings. Manufacturing quality is the effectiveness of the production processes in building products that are faithful to the design specifications, including reliability and durability. A more-precise term for manufacturing quality, therefore, is quality of conformance.

Design quality and manufacturing quality (quality of conformance) are equally important in product competitiveness. The best designs in the world are meaningless if the workmanship of the products is shoddy. Likewise, building products faithfully to lousy designs is no way to earn customer satisfaction.

Cost

Customers, to be precise, are interested in the prices that companies charge for products, not in the companies' manufacturing costs. But companies need to charge prices that are sufficient to cover their manufacturing costs. So companies' manufacturing costs per unit produced essentially determine the price competitiveness of their products.

Companies need to manage their costs with an eye to the price levels determined by the market rather than simply trying to charge sufficiently high prices for whatever their costs happen to total. They should start, that is, by determining the optimal price levels for their products in the marketplace and then work backwards: establish and pursue cost targets in R&D and in manufacturing that will allow for securing viable margins at competitive prices.

Manufacturing costs comprise labor cost, material cost, and expenses, including R&D expenses and depreciation expenses. To those costs we add selling, general, and administrative expenses to arrive at companies' overall operating costs. We can analyze each cost element per unit in regard to productivity and input prices. Labor cost per unit, for example, is the simple average of wages and salaries per hour (labor input) divided by unit production per person-hour (labor productivity). Note that raising productivity is the best way to lower unit costs over the long term. It is a sounder, more-sustainable approach than that of demanding wage concessions from labor and price concessions from suppliers.

Delivery

In regard to competitiveness, delivery refers to how long customers need to wait for the products they have purchased. Long waiting times for product delivery can nullify the appeal of high quality and low price.

Waiting times reflect production lead times and, for newly created products, development lead times. The buyer of a custom home, for example, needs to wait for the architect to create the design (development lead time) and then for the contractor to build the house (production lead time). Development lead time is irrelevant, meanwhile, to the person who purchases a mass-produced automobile in a make-to-order manufacturing format. He or she only needs to wait for the factory to fill the order (production lead time). And the person who buys a car in a showroom in a make-to-stock manufacturing format can drive it home today. He or she waits neither for the production lead time nor for the development lead time.

An important determinant of delivery lead time is the production capacity of the relevant production processes. Shortages in production capacity will cause increases in order backlog and delays in product delivery. So we should regard production capacity as a factor, albeit an indirect one, in competitiveness.

Flexibility

Markets today present rapidly shifting patterns of demand and unprecedented diversity in customer expectations. Flexibility—though of a different character from quality, cost, and delivery—therefore ranks with those three factors as a crucial determinant of competitiveness. It is an indicator of companies' ability to maintain their QCD-based competitiveness amid change in the operating environment.

For instance, measures for bolstering cost flexibility amid fluctuating production volumes might include minimizing fixed costs relative to variable costs and minimizing the cost of switching production between different items. Cost-flexibility measures for accommodating design changes might include sharing components among different product models and adapting production processes to produce multiple kinds of items.

People have traditionally regarded high flexibility and high productivity as mutually incompatible in manufacturing. But Japanese manufacturers—most notably Toyota—have succeeded in achieving both, and that success has become the wellspring of their international competitiveness.

Surface competitiveness and deep competitiveness

Figure 1-3 delineates capability-building competition in relation to surface competitiveness and earnings performance. Surface competition takes place in plain view of customers. Companies strive to outdo each other in appealing to customers through pricing, performance, reliability, availability, and service. Their surface competitiveness is the sum of the persuasiveness and the convincingness of the information that they package as products. Companies, of course, need to possess some minimum level of organizational capability and product quality to engage in that competition. But their competition centers on efforts to attain optimal combinations of unit sales volume and unit pricing to maximize profits.

Price competition is the most prominent form of surface competition. The concept of price competition is central to modern economic theory, and standard economics textbooks discuss competition largely in terms of pricing. Significantly, price competition does not necessarily include measures for strengthening companies' deep competitiveness.

Capability-building competition unfolds in the realm of organizational capability and in the deep-competition criteria of QCD&F. Companies refine their systems for supporting excellence in organizational routine. They benchmark each other's products and strive furiously to outdo one another in productivity and in other QCD&F criteria. Although the competition unfolds largely out of sight of consumers, the results of that competition determine a big part of companies' surface competitiveness—their product appeal in the eyes of customers and, consequently, their market share. Capability-building competition ultimately figures decisively in companies' profitability.

Efforts to build capabilities account for a big part of daily activity at Japanese automakers and auto parts manufacturers. Similar efforts are also evident at non-Japanese automakers. The author recalls a visit to a European vehicle plant in the mid-1990s. There, he saw a banner emblazoned with the slogan, "Let's improve assembly productivity to 17 person-hours per vehicle!" The figure of 17 person-hours per vehicle became famous through research findings published in 1990 by the Massachusetts Institute of Technology–based International Motor Vehicle Program. It was the average vehicle assembly productivity at Japanese automakers as calculated by the program researchers. Productivity in European vehicle assembly was still well below that level, and catching up with the Japanese became the interim target for European automakers.

Raising productivity requires sweeping and fundamental change. The European vehicle plant visited by the author needed to tackle change in its organization, process layout, equipment design, process control, work procedures, wage scales, even in its approach to motivating employees. That capability building is of little interest to consumers, who are primarily interested in how much car they can buy for how much money. But it is a pressing concern for manufacturers, and it commands growing attention in manufacturing industries worldwide.

A long-term quest

Capability-building competition is inherently long term. People at companies tackle improvements in deep competitiveness even though consumers pay little note to their efforts in the short term. They tackle those improvements because they believe that increased deep competitiveness will strengthen their customer appeal over the long term. They believe that it will improve their companies' prospects for survival.

The difficulty of overcoming gaps in deep competitiveness contrasts starkly with the ease of—at least temporarily—offsetting differentials in surface competitiveness. Manufacturers can always lower prices to competitors' price levels, though that might mean selling at below cost, an unsustainable stratagem. Similarly, they can match competitors' delivery lead times by amassing inventories. Strengthening deep competitiveness, however, depends on improvements in organizational capability. Those improvements require changes in basic systems, which can be difficult and even impossible to accomplish.

Overcoming a competitor's lead in deep competitiveness can thus be fiendishly difficult, even when management and employees recognize the problem. The author has been monitoring the deep competitiveness of automakers for some 20 years. Differentials among companies and among national industries in deep-competitiveness criteria, such as productivity and manufacturing quality, have proved stubborn. That observation reinforces the belief that we should regard differentials in deep competitiveness and in organizational capability as persistent characteristics rather than as short-term aberrations.

Backhanded evidence of the long-term character of deep competitiveness is apparent in the market's tolerance of competitive differentials. At least in the automotive sector, lagging behind competitors in productivity or in quality has not entailed immediate doom for the laggards. Stays of execution have been frequent and prolonged.

The realities of the automotive industry figure infrequently in mainstream economic models, which include an assumed equality in basic

FIGURE 1-3

Organizational Capability in Manufacturing and Corporate Performance

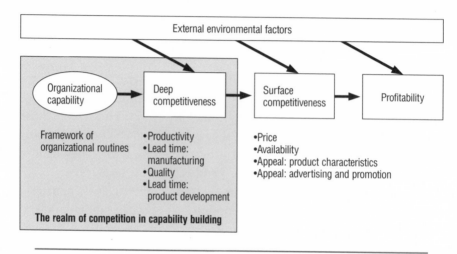

competitiveness. The modelers assume that market forces will oblige companies to keep up in capability building or that companies that fail to keep up will implode immediately. Their models—depictions of perfect price competition—fail to reflect the real-world mix of strong companies that are thriving and stragglers that are somehow getting by.

Differences between capability-building competition and price competition

Now that we have defined the basic scope of capability-building competition and of price competition, let us review the salient differences between the two.

Clarity of criteria

Pure price competition provides a singular, crystal-clear criterion for success or failure. Companies strive to offer products to customers "a mark, a yen, a buck, or a pound" cheaper than their competitors. Capability-building competition, on the other hand, is subject to multiple criteria, and which of those criteria warrant the highest priority over the long term can be difficult to ascertain.

People's consensus as to priorities in capability building is stronger in the automobile industry than in most other industries. But even the automotive sector leaves room for doubt about which competitive indicators to monitor most rigorously in analyzing competitors. Evaluation criteria can be vague, meanwhile, even in regard to indicators that clearly merit careful attention, such as productivity and manufacturing quality.

Difficulty of evaluating the strength of competitors accurately
Evaluating competitors' price competitiveness is basically as simple as looking at their window stickers or price tags. Evaluating their organizational capability or their deep competitiveness, however, requires more effort. And even the most assiduous benchmarking provides only rough approximations of productivity, lead time, quality, and other indicators of competitors' organizational capability and deep competitiveness.

Time required for response
Companies can respond immediately to pricing moves by their competitors, provided that covering costs is not a consideration. But responding to advantages asserted by competitors in deep competitiveness takes longer—a lot longer.

Potential for collusion
The danger of price collusion among ostensible competitors is an ever-present danger in the marketplace, but collusion in capability building is unheard of. The time and effort required to build capabilities makes capability-building collusion all but impossible, even with a small number of competitors—even with as few as only two competitors. If anything, the difficulty of gauging rivals' deep competitiveness stimulates competition. Companies tend to err on the side of amassing more capabilities than they require for the business at hand.

Controllability and emergence
Whereas pricing is subject to careful planning and fine-tuning, the process of capability building is far less controllable. Capability building frequently proceeds in wholly unexpected ways. Scientists refer to complex phenomena that arise unpredictably from simpler rules as emergent. In that sense, we can characterize capability building as an emergent process.

The process of capability building is a chaotic affair, and a capacity for persistent organizational learning is essential in promoting the emergence of competitive advantage through that process. The author discusses the resultant capabilities as evolved capabilities in chapter 5.

Collaboration and competition

Companies can shorten the time required to overcome competitors' advantages in capability building by undertaking joint projects with those competitors. Joint work on selected technologies, such as fuel cells or recycling technology, need not compromise rivals' overall competitive stance in surface competition. The companies can continue to compete vigorously in product pricing and specifications even as they cooperate in selected technologies. That combination of competition and cooperation is possible even when companies develop and produce vehicle models jointly; they can market competing versions of the same base vehicle.

Examples abound of companies engaging in price competition and other surface competition while they engage in deep, capability-building competition. That parallel competition is the rule in industrial sectors, like automobiles, that are subject to intense international competition. Companies fortify their organizational capability and strengthen their cost structure, their quality-assurance function, and other facets of their deep competitiveness through capability-building competition. Their progress in building capabilities underlies their continuing and intense competition in pricing and in other facets of surface competition.

Protectionist trade regimes and pervasive regulations, however, do nothing to stimulate capability-building competition. We see protected and heavily regulated sectors where companies only go through the motions of price competition or where they don't even bother with the pretense. The world's consumers have a vested interest in competition that prompts companies to strengthen their deep competitiveness and their surface competitiveness. That kind of competition encourages across-the-board improvements in organizational capability, which under-lies corporate competitiveness, and it thereby supports overall gains in customer satisfaction.

Capability-building competition, invisible to consumers, has been the defining trend in the world automobile industry since the mid-1970s. To be sure, differentials between automakers in profitability and in surface competitiveness reflected external factors, such as currency exchange rates, and company-specific factors, such as strategic blunders. But through everything, we witnessed a sustained, industrywide improvement in productivity, in manufacturing quality, and in other facets of deep competitiveness. And we have Toyota and other Japanese automakers to thank for leading the global, capability-building competition in production, product development, and purchasing.

2. Evolving Corporate Systems

The capability-building process

Capability building is a step-by-step process, and capability-building competition in the automobile industry reflects the evolutionary character of the industry. Economists and management theorists began using modern evolutionary theory in the 1960s to analyze change at corporations and in groups of corporations. Evolutionary theory has since become a widely used tool in the social sciences, especially since the 1980s.

We need to be careful, of course, in applying evolutionary concepts from biology to the utterly different disciplines of management, economics, and sociology. We need to be especially wary of crude social Darwinism, which rationalizes and condones the marginalization of the weaker members of society. Concepts drawn from modern evolutionary theory yield valuable insights, however, in dynamic and historic approaches to sociological research on companies.

Whether the subject is biological organisms or corporate organizations, evolutionary analysis elucidates stability and change—continuity and discontinuity—in systems. It explains how change occurs occasionally in systems that are inherently resistant to change. Evolutionary theory focuses on genes, which resist change and retain their identity faithfully over multiple generations, and on the mechanism of transferring genes between generations. The corporate equivalents of genes are organizational capability and its constituent elements, which we refer to collectively as organizational routine. The corporate equivalent of mutation in genes, meanwhile, is the emergence that we have cited in capability building.

Corporate evolutionary theory resembles its biological progenitor, too, in seeking reasons for the existence of rational, complex systems. Here, rational means fulfilling the conditions for survival. Corporations and organisms that have survived are, by this definition, rational. Complex means more complex than anything we would expect to arise by mere chance.

We need to remember, however, that evolutionary theory is utterly non-judgmental about the "good" or the "bad" of change in organisms. It explains that change entirely and exclusively in regard to accommodating environmental conditions. Evolution thus differs, strictly speaking, from progress toward some management ideal—"improvement"—which we might hope to see in corporations.

Biological evolutionary theory and its corporate scion are also similar in distinguishing between origin theory and continuation theory. Origin theory is a matter of elucidating the reasons for the changes that have spawned the systems under observation. Continuation theory rationalizes—after the fact—systems that have resulted from changes. Mainstream Darwinian theorists today account for the origin of species as the chance result of random mutations, and they account for the continuation of species as the result of natural selection.

Corporate organizations are social systems, and we therefore need to attribute some of the change that occurs in them to human intent. We cannot attribute that change entirely, that is, to random mutations, as we do in biological mutation. Nor, on the other hand, can we attribute that change entirely to conscious planning. We thus need to regard the evolution of corporate systems as a combination of chance and planning. The author characterizes that phenomenon as system emergence.

Capabilities: making things, making improvements, making progress

Organizational capability in regard to manufacturing comprises the three layers outlined in figure 1-4. The base layer is routine manufacturing capability. That is the capability of producing the same product as competitors at lower cost, at higher quality, and with shorter delivery lead time. (The author uses the word *routine* here and elsewhere in the positive sense of rigorous, conscientious consistency. His usage carries none of the connotations of "hackneyed" or "wearisome" sometimes associated with that word.)

The second layer of organizational capability is routine improvement capability: the ability to achieve continuing improvements—*kaizen*—in productivity, quality, delivery lead time, and other facets of deep competitiveness. That capability consists of an organizationally ingrained capacity and predilection for undertaking problem-solving cycles continually, which drives relentless improvement in products and in production processes.

Underlying routine manufacturing capability and routine improvement capability is the third layer: evolutionary capability; in other words, capability-building capability. That capability, anything but routine, is the capacity for tossing up new capabilities out of the soup of organizational chaos. It is the resilient capacity for learning from success and from failure, including a readiness to learn from the successes of others.

Evolving consumers

Consumers become increasingly demanding and sophisticated in their expectations of products. Demand evolves, just as supply-side organizations, products, and technology evolve. Japanese consumers formerly flocked to new vehicle models that excelled conspicuously in any facet of catalog specifications or that sported new features. Automakers could ensure strong sales by being first to market in a model class with conspicuous advances in such performance criteria as fuel economy or acceleration, for example, or with such features as double-overhead cams, full-time four-wheel drive, or turbochargers.

Japanese consumers have since learned to scrutinize cars more comprehensively and with more-nuanced eyes. Seeking the products that best match their lifestyles, they have become sensitive to overall balance in specifications and features. Car buyers in Japan now pursue a fidelity to their individual needs that the author calls product integrity.

Customer satisfaction is fleeting. Witness the restaurant, once the talk of the town, that loses its reputation and its diners after it allows quality to slip or after it stops making continual improvements in its menu. To retain customer satisfaction, companies need to work unceasingly through capability building to strengthen their product offerings and to fortify their overall competitiveness. That is the only way to keep up with the escalating expectations of increasingly perceptive customers. When

FIGURE 1-4

The Three Levels of Organizational Capability in Manufacturing

	Kind of routine	Kind of capability
Routine manufacturing capability	Repeatedly transferring information	Passive: repeatedly assert competitive advantage
Routine kaizen capability	Repeatedly solving problems	Active: increase competitive advantage
Evolutionary capability (capability-building capability)	Managing emergent capability building	Active: move faster than competitors in building capabilities in manufacturing and in kaizen routines

companies do their part, the result is a synergistic, tandem evolution in manufacturers' ability to identify and satisfy consumer needs and in consumers' ability to evaluate products.

3. Competition in Basic Design Concepts

The lack of revolutionary change in the basic design concept of the automobile

The author argues throughout this work that the automobile industry has grown and developed through competition in incremental capability building. That competition, however, has occasioned little change—certainly no revolution—in the basic design concept of the automobile.

We can identify two main aspects of design concept in products that comprise numerous components, whether automobiles or computers. One aspect is the selection of core component technologies. The other is the choice of product architecture; that is, how to put the parts together.

Competition among core component technologies

The engine is the core component technology in automobiles, just as the central processing unit and the operating system are the core component technologies in computers. We frequently see competition among multiple candidates for core component technologies when a new product category emerges. The first car powered with a gasoline internal combustion engine appeared in 1886, but steam power and electric power remained serious rivals to gasoline power in automobiles for another 20 years.

Gasoline famously emerged from that early-stage technological competition as the de facto standard for powering passenger cars, and the 20th century became the era of the gasoline-powered car. After two oil crises in the 1970s, people began to call in earnest for alternatives to gasoline power—for the reinvention, as it were, of the automobile. Gasoline retained its preeminence, however, as automakers used electronic control and other incremental improvements to make gasoline engines more energy efficient.

Fuel cells or another new technology might well unseat gasoline power sometime in the 21st century as the chief means of powering passenger cars. But this work focuses on events in the latter half of the 20th century, and the automobile industry was essentially devoid of real competition among core component technologies during that time span.

Competition among product architectures

Products that comprise numerous components are of two main kinds of architectures: integral and modular. In integral architecture, the principal components interact organically in complex ways. The functionality and performance of products depend heavily on designing and manufacturing every principal component to interact smoothly with the other components. So the manufacturers of the end products tend to rely mainly on components developed especially for their products. Automobiles are a classic example of integral product architecture. More than 90% of the components in a mass-production vehicle model are usable only in that model and in other models produced by the same automaker.

In modular architecture, the interaction among components occurs entirely through clear-cut interfaces. The makers of the end products can rely largely on off-the-shelf, commodity components, as long as the component interfaces—physical connections and digital syntax—adhere closely to industry standards. Personal computers are a good example of modular product architecture.

Note that cars were also a modular-architecture product in the early years of the automobile industry. Then, Henry Ford began assembling the Model T in 1908 from components designed especially for his product. His approach proved spectacularly successful, and integral architecture has prevailed in vehicle design and manufacturing ever since.

2 Why Cars?

In the previous chapter, we deployed concepts to help analyze capability-building competition in the world automobile industry. We now begin our analysis, starting with a question: Why were automobiles the sector where Japanese companies asserted their most pronounced international competitiveness? The concepts of product architecture and product integrity will prove invaluable in elucidating the answer.

1. Is Japan's Automobile Industry Truly Strong?

Numbers

Our first task is to verify whether Japan's automobile industry was really as strong as it appears to have been. That automobiles and auto parts were the preeminent manufacturing industry in Japan in the 1980s and 1990s is clear. The automotive sector accounted for between 10% and 15% of Japan's manufacturing output. It accounted for around 10% of capital spending and a similar percentage of R&D expenditures in Japan's private sector. Automobiles and auto parts earned about 20% of Japan's export revenues.

Japanese automakers' share of global vehicle production, only 0.3% in 1950 and less than 3% in 1960, had surged to 18% by 1970 and to 29% by 1980 (fig. 2-1). It peaked at nearly 35% in 1990 before slipping somewhat to just under 30% at the end of the century. Note that those figures include production at plants outside Japan, which increased rapidly in the 1980s and 1990s. Note, too, that the 1990s declines in Japanese automakers' domestic production and in their share of global production coincided with Japan's "lost decade" of economic stagnation.

In the 1990s, Japanese automakers had earned market shares of about 30% in North America and about 10% in the European Union. Their share was larger than 10%—even as large as around 30%—in several

19

FIGURE 2-1

Global Vehicle Production: All Automakers and Japanese Automakers (passenger cars and commercial vehicles; thousand vehicles)

	All automakers	Japanese automakers			
		In Japan	Overseas*	Total	Percentage of total
1950	10,580	30	—	30	0.3
1960	16,490	480	—	480	2.9
1970	29,400	5,290	—	5,290	18.0
1980	38,510	11,040	—	11,040	28.7
1990	48,280	13,490	3,380	16,870	34.9
2000	58,300	10,150	6,940	17,220	29.5

* The author has not presented figures for overseas production by the Japanese automakers before 1990 because precise data is unavailable and because the estimated numbers are inconsequential: fewer than 500,000 vehicles in 1980 and negligible numbers in the earlier years listed.
Sources: Jidosha Sangyo Handobukku (Automobile Industry Handbook), annual editions, Nikkan Jidosha Shimbunsha; other

European nations that do not have local automobile industries. In most of the principal automobile markets of Southeast Asia, the Japanese share ranged from 50% to 90%.

Qualitative measures of competitiveness

Japanese companies thus asserted a strong presence in the world automobile industry in the final quarter of the 20th century. Let us next examine their competitiveness during that period in regard to deep competitiveness, surface competitiveness, and profitability.

Benchmarking became a favored tool of industry researchers in the automotive sector in the 1980s. The emergence of the Japanese automakers as global competitors had heightened the intensity of competition in the industry. A North American, European, Japanese convergence was under way in vehicle size and in other elements of product concept. The U.S. Department of Transportation and other U.S. government agencies had employed benchmarking since the 1970s to monitor competitiveness. In the 1980s, researchers at U.S. universities, such as Harvard and MIT, became active in benchmarking competitiveness in the automobile industry, and international networks of industry researchers, including Japanese academics, took shape. An especially prominent example of that international networking was the MIT-based International Motor Vehicle Program.

The collaborative international research on competitiveness in the automobile industry in the 1980s and 1990s reflected the complex and incremental character of capability-building competition. That research was rare in its exhaustiveness. No example comes to mind readily of research of comparable scope and duration in any other industrial sector. In hindsight, universities were a fortuitous platform for conducting research on the international competitiveness of automakers. The research extended to indicators of deep competitiveness—productivity, quality, and lead time in R&D and in manufacturing—that automakers generally regard as confidential. As neutral observers, university researchers enjoyed far greater access to information than partisan observers ever could have obtained. Let us hope that researchers in the 21st century will carry on their groundbreaking work and build on their invaluable findings.

Deep competitiveness

Comparative studies of international competitiveness in the automobile industry in the 1980s and 1990s repeatedly produced similar conclusions: that Japanese vehicle assemblers, on average, excelled their U.S. and European counterparts in assembly productivity, manufacturing quality, product-development lead time, product-development productivity, and other indicators of deep competitiveness. To be sure, determined efforts enabled some of the U.S. and European automakers to narrow the competitiveness gap in some indicators of deep competitiveness. And the appreciation of the yen offset part of the Japanese edge in cost competitiveness. Yet the research findings stated unanimously that the Japanese retained their overall edge in manufacturing and product-development performance at century-end.

Manufacturing productivity

We have a choice of measures of productivity at automakers and at their individual factories, including value-added productivity, total factor productivity, and physical productivity. The latter, physical productivity, provides the most direct measurement of workplace capabilities, so we will focus on that measure.

Several small-scale studies in the 1980s illuminated Japanese leadership in productivity in the flagship process of automobile manufacturing: vehicle assembly. Then, the International Motor Vehicle Program (IMVP) confirmed that leadership convincingly through its comprehensive comparative survey of productivity in passenger car assembly worldwide. The IMVP survey measured the number of person-hours required per standard vehicle for body welding, body painting, and whole-vehicle assembly work.

Here's how the survey measured physical productivity. Assume that 1,000 workers at a vehicle assembly plant produced 400 vehicles per eight-hour workday. The survey would measure physical productivity there as 20 person-hours per vehicle: 1,000 people × 8 hours (8,000 person-hours) ÷ 400 vehicles = 20 person-hours/vehicle. The lower the figure for person-hours per vehicle, the higher the productivity. To help ensure meaningful comparisons, the survey compensated for different levels of robotization and different levels of difficulty in the assembly work.

The IMVP released its survey findings in 1989. Those findings indicated, as noted in the previous chapter, that Japanese plants assembled vehicles in an average of 17 person-hours per vehicle. In contrast, the average was 25 person-hours per vehicle at U.S. plants and 37 person-hours per vehicle at European plants. The Americans and Europeans were understandably alarmed. Just how alarmed became evident in follow-up survey findings released in 1993. The Americans had improved their average productivity to 23 person-hours per vehicle, and the Europeans had achieved an even-bigger improvement, to 26 person-hours per vehicle. Japan's vehicle plants, on the other hand, had reduced their person-hours per vehicle only one hour, to 16. Bear in mind, however, that national averages can be deceiving. Japan's best vehicle assembly plants produced passenger cars in only 13 person-hours per vehicle, and the least-productive Japanese plants were less efficient than the best U.S. plants.

We also need to consider physical productivity industrywide, including productivity in automotive components manufacturing. The author and Akira Takeishi, a professor at Hitotsubashi University, used statistical data to calculate productivity from that standpoint in Japanese and U.S. industries. They examined data for years when capacity utilization was high: 1990 in Japan and 1988 in the United States. They found that physical productivity in the automobile industry was 131 person-hours per vehicle in Japan and 152 person-hours per vehicle in the United States. The productivity differential between Japan and the United States thus appears to be smaller in the automobile industry overall than in vehicle assembly. Other evidence also suggests that Japanese manufacturers' greatest strength is in assembly manufacturing, a subject to which we will return.

Interestingly, labor productivity in the Japanese automobile industry essentially stopped rising in the 1980s. It edged up only 0.3% annually in that decade after climbing 6% per year in the 1970s.

Assiduous efforts at U.S. and European automakers enabled them to narrow the physical-productivity gap with their Japanese counterparts. The Japanese automakers, however, also continued to raise their physical productivity—more than 20% in the latter half of the 1990s alone. In the year 2000, average physical productivity thus remained higher in Japan than in the United States or in Europe. That reinforces our perception that overcoming a differential in deep competitiveness is a long-term challenge. It depends, as we have seen, on fundamental improvement in the formidable realm of organizational capability.

Manufacturing lead time

The author is unaware of any conclusive survey findings about Japanese superiority in manufacturing lead time. But the industry consensus is that Japanese automakers outrace their U.S. and European counterparts in transforming materials into vehicles. A useful indicator of manufacturing lead time is the turnover rate for work-in-process inventory, and Japanese automakers display higher work-in-process turnover rates than their U.S. counterparts. Toyota, famed for its just-in-time production, has traditionally ranked notably high in work-in-process turnover.

U.S. and European automakers have emulated the Toyota Production System, and their work-in-process turnover rates have risen as a result. But they remain less efficient than Toyota and Japan's other efficiency leaders. Survey results indicate, meanwhile, that U.S. auto parts makers have lagged their vehicle-assembling customers in shrinking inventories.

Manufacturing quality

Publications and market research firms began releasing comparisons of vehicle quality in the United States in the 1980s. The U.S. market is the scene of the most wide-open competition among the world's automakers, and the surveys received extensive attention in the mass media and among consumers. Two widely cited examples are the Predicted Reliability Rating by *Consumer Reports* magazine and the Initial Quality Study by the market research firm J.D. Power and Associates. *Consumer Reports* prepares its Predicted Reliability Rating on the basis of long-term data, whereas J.D. Power's Initial Quality Study covers the rate of complaints by new-car owners in the first 90 days of ownership.

The survey results confirmed an edge for the Japanese automakers over their U.S. and European counterparts in manufacturing quality. Japanese models, along with a handful of luxury models from German manufacturers, dominated the top end of the rankings. That trend affected the purchasing decisions of American consumers greatly, and the annual quality rankings became a source of joy and consternation for the automakers, depending on their performance. All of the automakers strove mightily to raise their standing in the rankings—yet another kind of capability-building competition.

Spurred by the Japanese, the U.S. and European automakers made impressive gains in manufacturing quality. The quality gap, like the productivity gap, narrowed. But as in productivity, the Japanese automakers also made gains in quality, and they retained their overall lead in that phase of capability building, too.

Competition in the quality phase of capability building is an eternal challenge for every automaker. As quality standards rise, consumers become more sophisticated and more demanding. Automakers' reward for success in improving their manufacturing quality is demand from consumers for further improvement.

Development productivity and lead time
The focus of competition in the automobile industry has broadened since the late 1980s to encompass productivity and lead time in product development, as well as productivity and quality in assembly manufacturing. In the process, the U.S. and European automakers have had a rude awakening. They have discovered that the conventional wisdom—that the Japanese competitive edge was confined to manufacturing—was dead wrong. Japan's automakers have asserted a commanding edge, overall, in developing products quickly and efficiently.

In the 1980s, the author and other researchers at Harvard University surveyed lead times from product conceptualization—traditionally equated with the first product-planning meeting—to showroom launch. The survey results indicated that the average lead time was about four years at the Japanese automakers and about five years at the U.S. automakers. They indicated that the average lead time from the decision on the basic exterior design to the showroom launch was 30 months at the Japanese automakers and 40 months at the U.S. and European automakers. The survey revealed that the Japanese were faster than their U.S. and European counterparts in every phase of development, including the development of stamping dies and the fabrication of vehicle prototypes.

Even bigger than the difference in development lead times was the difference in development productivity. The survey results indicated that the Japanese automakers expended an average of 1.7 million person-hours per development project and that the U.S. and European automakers expended an average of 3.0 million. An advantage in development productivity enables automakers to launch more vehicle models than their competitors for the same amount of R&D spending. That is especially important in the automobile industry, where new models account for a disproportionately large percentage of sales. In fact, the Japanese, U.S., and European automakers spent roughly equal sums on product development from 1982 to 1987, and that spending spawned some 70 new models for the Japanese automakers, compared with only about 20 for the Americans and about 40 for the Europeans.

The Americans and the Europeans took the hint. They spent the 1990s playing catch-up with the Japanese in R&D speed and productivity. Their efforts included reorganizing their R&D organizations along Japanese lines and adopting the latest technology for computer-aided design. The U.S. automakers were notably successful. They appeared to have largely closed the gap on the Japanese by the mid-1990s. But their improving sales performance seems to have engendered complacency. The Japanese, on the other hand, gained a sense of urgency as they saw their advantage in financial performance slipping away. They responded by employing information technology aggressively—and effectively—to shorten their lead time further in product development.

Ultimately, the Japanese automakers padded their lead in the race to shorten development lead time, and they remained more than twice as productive as their U.S. and European competitors, on average, in product development. That is the finding of surveys by the author and his colleagues.

Manufacturing cost

Competitiveness in manufacturing cost is a composite of productivity and inputs—wages, raw materials, energy, logistics, etc. Input costs are subject to external factors, notably currency exchange rates, that are unrelated to basic capabilities in manufacturing. By the mid-1990s, the manufacturing costs for small cars produced in the United States and in Japan were roughly equal. That was despite Japan's demonstrable advantage in productivity. It reflected the strong yen—then around ¥100 to the dollar. It also reflected Japan's high-cost economic infrastructure, which inflates the cost of such manufacturing inputs as energy and logistics.

The first studies to detail convincingly a Japanese cost advantage in automobile manufacturing were at the outset of the 1980s. That was when the yen was far weaker relative to the dollar than it would later become. It was a time when Japan's automakers reportedly earned nearly all of their profits in North America. The survey findings were by the U.S. Department of Transportation and by Harvard University. They revealed that Japan enjoyed a cost advantage over the United States of between $1,000 and $2,000 in producing an equivalent small car. Most of that cost advantage consisted of lower labor costs: lower wages and higher labor productivity.

Japan's cost advantage deteriorated rapidly as the 1980s wore on. The Plaza Accord of 1985 produced a sharp upward revaluation of the yen. Productivity-raising efforts by the U.S. automakers yielded results, and the booming U.S. economy supported increasing economies of scale. Productivity gains slowed, meanwhile, at the Japanese automakers.

Surface competitiveness

Japanese automakers' compelling advantages in deep competitiveness have not necessarily translated consistently into comparable advantages in surface competitiveness. Let's take a look at the chimeras of pricing, product appeal, and sales and service.

Price competitiveness

Movements in currency exchange rates inevitably affect the price competitiveness of exporters. In the mid-1990s, each ¥1 appreciation of the yen against the dollar cost the Japanese automobile industry hundreds of millions of dollars. Nor did shifting production overseas provide a failsafe hedge against currency risk. Japanese automakers in the United Kingdom, for example, suffered huge exchange losses in Europe in the early 2000s. That resulted from the weakening of the pound against the euro.

Exporters can absorb some of the effect of adverse movement in exchange rates by incurring exchange losses. But that is a stopgap. Sooner or later, they need to raise their prices. Witness the experience of the Japanese automakers in the U.S. market in the mid-1990s. The yen appreciated to less than ¥100 to the dollar, and midsized Japanese imports became about $2,000 more expensive per vehicle than comparable American models.

Interestingly, the strong yen proved less than devastating for Japanese car sales in the United States. Part of the reason was the increase in local production by the Japanese automakers. Another big reason, however, was the excellent reputation for quality that the Japanese automakers had earned. Thanks to superior quality, Japanese cars retained their value better than American cars in the used-car market. That justified a premium in new-car sticker prices in the eyes of discriminating consumers. An advantage in the deep competitiveness of manufacturing quality and productivity thus carried over, albeit indirectly, to the surface competitiveness of pricing.

The best-selling Japanese models in the United States in the mid-1990s were the Honda Accord and Toyota Camry. Three-year-old Accords and Camrys retained more than 50% of their original value in the used-car market. Comparable American models retained just 30-some percent of their value. An Accord or a Camry purchased new for $20,000 was therefore worth more than $10,000 after three years, whereas a comparable American model purchased for $18,000 was worth only $6,000 or so.

Product appeal

Pricing aside, a vehicle's appeal in the eyes of consumers is a composite of the design quality of performance, handling, comfort, safety, and styling and the manufacturing quality of reliability and durability. Japanese automakers have earned high regard overall for manufacturing quality. Consumer evaluation of design quality, however, has varied greatly by maker and by model, even in the Japanese camp. And consumer perceptions of overall product appeal have varied accordingly.

Design quality and overall product appeal are notoriously difficult to gauge objectively. But the best available indications suggest a huge disparity in product appeal, even among the Japanese automakers, by the 1980s. The author and colleagues conducted a survey of models from 20 Japanese, U.S., and European automakers at the end of the decade. They gathered data about customer satisfaction, manufacturing quality, design quality, and fluctuations in long-term market share. Then, they analyzed the correlation among those criteria and ranked the automakers by overall product appeal. Some of the Japanese automakers placed alongside the German manufacturers of luxury cars at the top of the rankings. Others, however, placed at the low end of the rankings.

The primary weaknesses of the Japanese cars were their unexciting exterior and interior styling and their lack of strong brand identities. Those weaknesses were notably debilitating in the European market, where consumer demand for sophisticated styling and for distinctive brand character is especially strong. The Japanese automakers' small market share in Europe, of course, also reflected France's and Italy's de facto quantitative quotas on Japanese vehicle imports. But the message was clear: Developing models distinctive enough to capture the imagination of European consumers was a pressing issue for the Japanese automakers.

We should note that the Japanese automakers' overall product appeal tended upward throughout the 1980s. Supported by Japan's bubble economy, the nation's automakers strove mightily and successfully to achieve performance, design, and brand identities comparable to those of European luxury cars. Their zealousness spawned the excessive cost of over design, but they corrected that excess in the mid-1990s. And at the outset of the 21st century, the Japanese automakers are strengthening their brand identities even as they continue to simplify their designs.

Sales and service
No automaker has asserted a compelling competitive edge in sales and service internationally by exporting successful practices from its home

nation. Japan's automakers, for example, have long served their home market with a high-cost, high-service approach to sales and customer care. That approach includes a heavy reliance on inefficient door-to-door visitation. Having accustomed customers to excessive service, the automakers are stuck with that model. No automaker can afford to begin skimping on service as long as competitors continue to lavish attention on customers.

Productivity in Japanese vehicle retailing is thus extremely low. Vehicle sales per salesperson in Japan average only about four vehicles a month, compared with the U.S. average of about seven a month. The gap between Japanese and U.S. sales productivity is even bigger in urban markets. Japanese salespersons, however, are far more knowledgeable about the products they handle than their counterparts at most U.S. dealerships, and they earn far more trust among their customers. The quality of vehicle service, too, tends to be far higher in Japan than in the United States. Even Saturn, General Motors' division famed in the United States for standout customer service, was a nonstarter in Japan.

Japanese automakers have adopted some elements of Japanese-style service in luxury-car sales channels in the United States. But the traditional Japanese approach to sales and service shows no sign of taking hold widely in the U.S. market. Nor are Japanese consumers likely to accept U.S.-style low-cost, low-service approaches anytime soon in markets for big-ticket items, like automobiles. Internet retailing, which eliminates personal contact with customers, has been especially slow to take hold in Japan's vehicle market.

Japanese automakers' low profitability

The Japanese automakers' performance in surface competitiveness has been, as we have seen, spotty. Japan's automakers, however, have retained a consistent edge over their U.S. and European competitors in deep competitiveness. As a group, they assert impressive competitiveness overall. Which raises a question: Why is their profitability so low?

Profitability varies hugely among the Japanese automakers. But it has been consistently lower at all of them than their deep competitiveness would lead us to expect. That includes Toyota and Honda, two companies known in the Japanese industry for relatively high profitability.

In the early 1980s, the Japanese automakers were losing money in Japan and were making lots of money on exports to North America. The red ink in Japan resulted from price cutting necessitated by escalating competition and from increased subsidies to dealers to offset losses on their high-service, high-cost retailing. In North American business, the Japanese automakers' profitability benefited from the weak yen—more than ¥200 to the dollar—and from the nominally voluntary restraint in Japanese vehicle exports to the United States. That restraint, instituted in 1981, had the effect of raising prices for Japanese vehicles by artificially constraining supply. American consumers thus ended up subsidizing vehicle purchases by Japanese consumers.

The yen's sharp appreciation after the Plaza Accord of 1985 sapped the profitability of Japanese vehicle exports to the United States. As if in compensation, the Japanese automakers' profitability in their domestic market improved. Sales of expensive, highly configured cars surged amid the spending frenzy of Japan's economic bubble, which began in 1987. Profitability on exports subsequently increased, too, as the yen weakened somewhat and as the Japanese automakers made improvements in the profitability of their products and operations. And at the end of the 1980s, the Japanese automakers enjoyed a period of dual profitability in Japan and overseas. They posted aggregate pretax profits of ¥1 trillion, not including special items, in 1989. Their average pretax return on sales that year reached about 5%.

Returns on domestic and overseas business deteriorated after 1990. Japan's economic bubble burst, marking the beginning of what would be a decade of domestic economic stagnation. And the renewed strengthening of the yen again undercut profitability in export business. By 1993, aggregate pretax earnings at Japan's automakers had slumped to just ¥200 billion, and pretax return on sales had declined to only about 1%. The automakers had failed to build a domestic business that would generate profits in ordinary economic conditions. They had relied on export earnings to compensate for that shortcoming. And they had allowed the unnatural profitability of the economic bubble to obscure the problem. Now, the time of reckoning had arrived.

Japan's automakers, to their credit, took matters in hand. They reduced costs, mainly by simplifying product designs, to counter the adverse effect of the strong yen on earnings. And they tweaked their sales, service, and distribution practices in Japan to bolster profitability there. Their efforts and results were genuinely impressive. The strong yen cost Toyota, for example, around ¥100 billion a year in fiscal 1994 and 1995. Yet Japan's largest automaker succeeded in at least offsetting that loss through cost reductions. The other Japanese automakers were similarly successful in trimming costs to cope with the shift in currency exchange rates. They were cashing in on the reserves of over design that they had accumulated through years of furious competition. Their accumulated excesses in product specifications gave them the latitude to simplify product designs without diminishing their product appeal significantly.

Successful measures for reducing product costs paid off in spades for the Japanese automakers when the yen weakened again in 1996. Aggregate pretax profits in the Japanese automobile industry, net of special items, returned to ¥1 trillion, and the average pretax return on sales climbed back to more than 4%. The yen appreciated again in 1999 and 2000, but the operational improvements in Japan shielded the automakers' earnings, and overall profitability fared better than in the mid-1990s.

Strategic miscalculations

Notwithstanding impressive work in buttressing profitability, Japan's automakers posted generally low earnings in the 1980s and 1990s relative to their deep competitiveness. That was partly the result of the recurring appreciation of the yen. It also reflected the unprofitable character of Japanese marketing—a problem the industry only began to address in the mid-1990s. But we also need to recognize the effect of strategic miscalculations in undercutting profitability.

Japan's automakers created problems for themselves in diverse ways in the 1990s. An obsession with increasing sales volume is evident in several instances. Also clearly discernible in several instances is weakness in strategic planning.

Structurally low profitability, as we have seen, characterized the entire Japanese automobile industry. So a strategic blunder was often enough to push an automaker into the red. But none of the red ink that discolored any Japanese automaker's financial performance resulted from deteriorating organizational capability. All of the Japanese automakers retained fundamentally strong organizational capability in such core functions as product development, manufacturing, and purchasing.

In comparison with U.S. and European automakers

The U.S. and European automakers retained generally high profitability in the 1980s and 1990s. In contrast with their Japanese counterparts, they enjoyed that profitability despite their weakness in deep competitiveness. We need to recognize, however, the evanescence of profits at the U.S. automakers. The Big Three have historically swung between huge losses and huge profits in approximately 10-year cycles. Their earnings volatility is far greater than that of the Japanese automakers. That is counter to what their lower dependence on exports—and their correspondingly smaller exposure to exchange rate fluctuations—would lead us to expect. The Big Three export less than 10% of the vehicles that they produce in the United States, whereas Japanese automakers export nearly one-half of the vehicles that they produce in Japan.

Much of the earnings volatility at the U.S. automakers and at the European automakers is attributable to their strategic orientation. Managements gear their companies toward milking the greatest-possible profits from economic upturns. That aspect of their strategy has been generally successful, but the U.S. and European automakers are less adept at coping with market downturns. They lack the kind of reserve strength that the Japanese automakers draw on to cope with adverse business conditions. And their fragility in the face of weakening demand or escalating competition subjects them to periodic floods of red ink.

Toyota, a Japanese leader in fiscal performance, has not displayed conspicuously high profitability over the long term by U.S. and European standards. But it has been astoundingly consistent in remaining profitable. Toyota last posted an after-tax loss in 1950. It remained profitable, that is, every year throughout the latter half of the 20th century, and it has retained that momentum in the 21st century. Honda has been similarly consistent, having remained profitable on a full-year basis every year since its establishment.

Toyota, Honda, and the other Japanese automakers have faced severe trials, such as the oil crises and sharp upturns in the value of the yen. But they have summoned sufficient fortitude in their manufacturing, in their product development, and in their other core functions to cope with those challenges.

2. Japanese Cars and Japanese Companies

Why Japan's automakers are so strong

We have seen that manufacturing is basically a matter of transferring design information to physical media. So we can regard manufacturing productivity as manufacturers' efficiency in transferring that information, manufacturing quality as their precision in transferring the information, and manufacturing lead time as the speed of the transference. Similarly, we can regard productivity, quality, and lead time in product development as efficiency, precision, and speed in translating market information and technological information into new products.

History records that Japanese automakers and some other Japanese manufacturers emerged as world leaders in the latter half of the 20th century. What history does not record clearly is why Japanese manufacturers became internationally competitive in some sectors and not in others. Since we understand manufacturing as the transference of information, we should seek the answer to that question in the informational characteristics of the products in the sectors in question.

Design information: rubbing things together

Product architecture is a definitive means of categorizing products, whether we regard the products as assemblies of physical components or as arrangements of information. Modular architecture, as we saw in chapter 1, brings together components that interact entirely through clear-cut interfaces. It allows for using off-the-shelf, commodity components. Modular architecture simply requires that the component interfaces—physical connections and digital syntax—adhere closely to industry standards. It therefore tends to conform with our notion of open architecture.

Integral architecture, on the other hand, brings together components that interact organically in complex ways. Product functionality and performance depend heavily on designing and manufacturing every principal component to interact smoothly with the other components. The author

FIGURE 2-2

Product Architecture as Functional Design and Structural Design

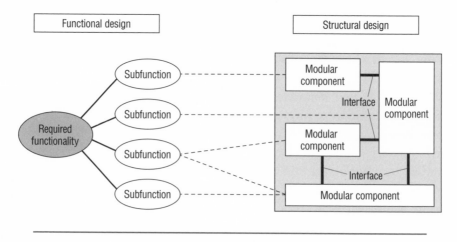

characterizes the work of creating components for integral-architecture products and of assembling those components into finished products as "rubbing things together." Manufacturers of integral-architecture products, as noted in chapter 1, rely mainly on components developed especially for their products. Integral architecture tends to conform to what we regard as closed architecture.

Modular architecture

Figure 2-2 presents an example of product architecture where each component module corresponds to a discrete function. Each module is a self-contained unit for performing its function. Only minimal exchange of information and energy among the modules is necessary for the modules to function smoothly.

The designers of modular products require only a good basic understanding of the rules for interfacing among the modules. They do not require in-depth knowledge of the individual modules to design excellent products. Nor do the designers of the modules need to think much about how the other modules work.

Integral architecture

In integral product architecture, the relationships between functionality and components are complex and overlapping. Epitomizing this architecture is the automobile. Each vehicle function straddles multiple components. For example, the tires, suspension, shock absorbers, chassis, body, engine, transmission, and numerous other components all figure in riding comfort. Overall comfort will suffer significantly if any of these interacting components is the least bit out of kilter.

Integral-architecture products typically include a lot of components that figure in multiple functions. The vehicle body, for instance, is a decisive factor in safety, comfort, styling, aerodynamics, and other crucial functions.

Whereas creating modular products is largely a matter of putting blocks neatly together, creating integral products is a messier process. Thus the author's characterization of that process as "rubbing things together."

Open and closed architecture

The functionality of modular components is readily available to any assembly manufacturer, but modular product architecture can be either closed or open in regard to company relationships (fig. 2-3). Manufacturing desktop computers, a quintessentially modular product category, is a wide-open business characterized by free-wheeling interchange among the participating companies. In contrast, IBM asserted unilateral control over the functional design of its legendary 360 mainframe computer even while employing a highly modular architecture.

Integral product architecture, on the other hand, is generally closed architecture in regard to the relationships among the participating companies. Sedan-type passenger cars feature a tightly closed architecture. A single company, the vehicle assembler, assumes unilateral control over the basic functional design and over the interfacing among the components.

Sectors where Japanese companies are strong

Japanese manufacturers emerged as world leaders in sectors where competition centers on capabilities in transferring design information to media. Few have asserted compelling international competitiveness in sectors where modular architecture minimizes the importance of those

FIGURE 2-3
Closed/Open, Integral/Modular Architecture

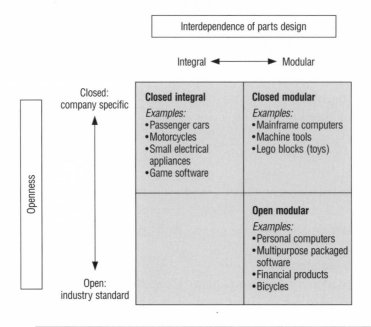

capabilities. Japanese companies are also notably absent among the global leaders in service industries.

The distinction between manufacturing and service sectors warrants some consideration in the context of product media. Commentators have traditionally distinguished between manufacturing and service sectors in reference to the durability of the media. They have regarded manufactured products as durable media that allow for—require—stocking in inventories, and they have regarded services as ephemeral media consumed immediately at the point of sale.

Digitization has rendered obsolete the traditional media-centric distinction between goods and services. That distinction was already under strain even before the digital age dawned. We were to regard a commercial song as a service, for example, if we paid to hear it in a club and as a manufactured good if we paid to obtain it on the tangible media of a vinyl record. Now, the commercial songs purchased over the Internet defy the traditional distinction entirely.

FIGURE 2-4

Permanent/Evanescent Media, Resistant/Receptive to Information Transfer

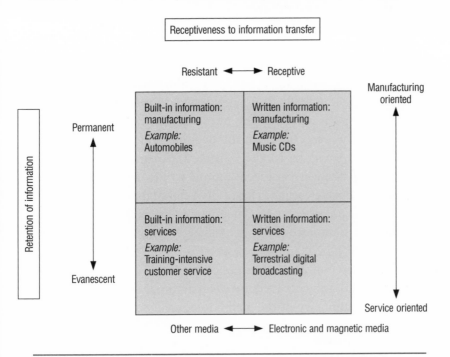

Figure 2-4 presents two more-useful criteria for categorizing industries in the digital era; namely, the difficulty of transferring design information to the product media and the evanescence of the design information. At the upper right in the figure are industries, like music distributors, who vend easily reproduced information in durable formats.

Our main product interest in this book, the automobile, presents huge challenges in transferring information to media and retains the information well. In contrast, digital terrestrial television broadcasts require essentially no artifice in processing the product information for sale, and the information—as sold—has no physical durability whatsoever.

Services that center on personal communication, such as in-store retailing, are also evanescent in terms of product life span. Customers consume services as they make their purchases. The media in these business models are the employees who provide the services. And transferring design information to employees through training and education is a huge and continuing task. Capabilities in human resources development are a decisive competitive criterion in personal-service retailing.

Characteristics of automotive architecture

The automobile began life in the late 19th century as an open-architecture product. Inventive individuals created the early motor vehicles largely from standard parts intended for horse-drawn carriages or bicycles. Henry Ford, however, converted the fledgling industry irreversibly to closed architecture with his Model T. By the 1990s, more than 90% of the parts in most passenger cars were unique to the cars' manufacturers. Accompanying the increasingly closed character of the automobile was an increasingly integral orientation. That integral orientation has been especially apparent in monocoque-body passenger cars, and those cars have been the forte of Japan's automakers.

The reader deserves an accounting of how we can measure just how integral or modular the architecture of an automobile or any product is. Here is a brief summary of the methodology employed by the author's research group.

An automobile encompasses about 10 basic systems, such as power train, body, chassis, interior, etc. It comprises dozens of subsystems and a thousand or so functional components. Altogether, some 30,000 nuts, bolts, and other parts make up a finished automobile.

We analyze each functional component and characterize it as model specific (designed for and used in only a single model family); company specific (designed for and used in multiple models produced by the same automaker); or industry standard (used in multiple models produced by different automakers). We make this characterization separately for the functional components and for the peripheral "interface" components used to link functions in the overall vehicle architecture.

In figure 2-5, we find industry-standard components and interfaces in such categories as spark plugs, batteries, and replacement tires. Industry-standard functional components fitted with model-specific interfaces are especially common in electromechanical items, like starters and alternators. That reflects the need for accommodating space constraints in engine compartments of different configurations.

FIGURE 2-5

Examples of Industry-Standard, Automaker-Specific, and Model-Specific Parts and Part Interfaces

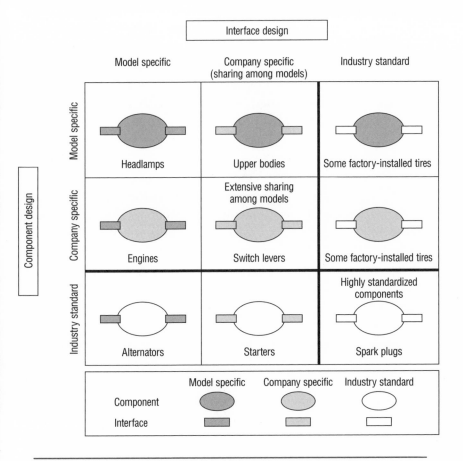

Model-specific or company-specific components fitted with industry-standard interfaces occur in numerous product categories. Typical are the original-equipment tires developed and supplied by tire manufacturers for individual model families. The metal wheels—interfaces—on which the tires are installed are generally of configurations that accommodate similar vehicles from all automakers. We find model-specific components and model-specific interfaces in product categories essential to evoking model identity, such as exterior trim and interior furnishings.

Next, we obtain a rough approximation of the openness of the architecture. We do that by calculating the percentage of industry-standard components in the total number of functional components and interface components. What we find is that the percentage of industry-standard components in a typical automobile is less than 10%. The percentage is higher than 30% in most electrical appliances and is higher than 50% in most personal computers. Meanwhile, the percentage of model-specific components in a new vehicle model is typically between 60% and 80%. These figures show convincingly, albeit roughly, that vehicles feature a comparatively closed and highly integral architecture.

Hunks of steel

We have seen that products are packaged information, and in automobiles, the packaging is steel. Some early automobiles inherited wooden bodies from their horse-drawn forebears. But the sealed bodies of steel developed by General Motors and other automakers soon became dominant. The oil crises of the 1970s stimulated a lot of talk of a wholesale shift to lighter materials, especially in the United States. That talk reflected the Big Three U.S. automakers' determination to preserve the heavy weighting of big cars in U.S. vehicle sales. It subsided, however, as consumer demand obliged even the Big Three to downsize their model lines and as escalating competition diminished the appeal of expensive new materials.

To be sure, the amount of plastic and aluminum in automobiles has increased, but it remains modest. A mainstream Japanese passenger car model studied by the author was 75% steel, by weight, in 1975, and that percentage had declined only slightly, to 70%, in 2000.

The reliance on steel as the main material in automobiles, if it continues, will shape the automobile industry definitively. One, it will require the industry to retain its focus on large-volume production. That will happen even as automakers employ flexible manufacturing to accommodate individual customer needs and wants. It will happen because the physics and the economics of steel are unsuited to small-volume production.

Two, it will ensure that organizational capabilities in building functionality and customer appeal into vehicles will remain the chief determinant of automakers' competitiveness. That is because transferring design information to steel is extremely difficult and demands highly integrated manufacturing. A vibrant, smoothly functioning workplace is crucial in imprinting information on steel products effectively, and the Toyota Production System and other management systems that mobilize the workplace effectively will thus continue to set the pace for the automobile industry.

The same properties of steel that mandate large-volume production and effective workplace management demand effective tools for transferring design information to the steel. Foremost among those tools are stamping dies and advanced machine tools. Interestingly, Japan has the world's largest concentration of internationally competitive manufacturers in both of those product sectors.

Steel's properties also underlie the crucial importance of close coordination between the product design function and the manufacturing workplace. The difficulty of processing steel amplifies the penalty incurred by difficult-to-manufacture designs. It imparts a competitive advantage to companies that excel at creating designs that are easy to manufacture. Here again, Japanese automakers lead the industry in so-called design-for-manufacture capabilities. And that is largely because of the good communication between their product designers and their managers and supervisors in the manufacturing workplace.

What remains, what doesn't

The threat of a "hollowing" of Japanese industry is a much-discussed subject in Japan. Numerous Japanese fear that core manufacturing industries will depart for other climes, as they did in the United States. Commonly cited reasons for that fear include the appreciation of the yen, the mounting competition from newly emerging economies, and the aging and shrinking of the Japanese population.

Understanding products as media infused with information casts the mooted hollowing of industry in a somewhat different light. We see that Japan is likely to retain a competitive edge in industries that depend heavily on skills in transferring information to media. Japan's competitiveness is especially resilient in the automotive sector. That is because of the strengths that we have been discussing, such as good coordination between the design and manufacturing functions and industry-leading capabilities in information-transfer tools, like stamping dies and machine tools.

Manufacturers will abandon Japan for lower-wage nations in sectors where automation and other technological advances have eliminated the competitive importance of worker dexterity. Japan is even less likely to attain or retain an edge in industries where the very process of information transfer precludes differentiation. Packaged software for personal computers is a striking example. The process of transferring the product information—software programs—to media such as CD-ROM disks and the like is simple and undemanding. It offers essentially no latitude for asserting a competitive edge.

The competition to differentiate packaged software products advantageously occurs almost entirely in the design phase of production. Creativity in conceiving utterly new product ideas is of the essence, and Japanese software companies, notwithstanding some notable exceptions, have proved inferior to their U.S. counterparts in that regard.

Regional characteristics in organizational capability

We discover distinctive regional characteristics in the organizational capability of automakers. And we find only three consistently high-margin business models in the automobile industry at the end of the 20th century: the German automakers' high-performance luxury cars for the global market, the U.S. automakers' pickup trucks and sport-utility vehicles for the North American market, and the Japanese automakers' passenger cars for the North American market.

A modular-architecture orientation has been evident in the U.S. automakers' business model since the days of Henry Ford's Model T. That orientation supported highly profitable business as the General Motors of Alfred Sloan developed a full model line based on shared parts and began the practice of making periodic model changes. It remained a profitable approach in the large cars of the 1970s and in the pickups and SUVs of the 1990s.

In Germany, Daimler-Benz (now DaimlerChrysler) and BMW profited handsomely with high-performance luxury cars based on integral architecture. They underpinned their profitability with commanding strengths in design integrity and in brand building. Japan's automakers, led by Toyota, thrived largely on the strength of excellence in manufacturing integrity.

The geographical aspect of profitability remains a revealing indicator of the competitiveness of different business models in the automobile industry. It warrants careful attention in monitoring competitive dynamics in the industry in the 21st century.

3 The Anatomy of Organizational Capability in Manufacturing

Three features define the international competitiveness that the Japanese automakers and other Japanese companies had built in manufacturing by the 1980s. One, they overcame traditional tradeoffs in manufacturing and in product development and reconciled high productivity, high quality, and short lead time. Two, they achieved unprecedented flexibility in minimizing the cost increases associated with deploying extensive product portfolios, with accommodating fluctuations in production volumes, and with introducing new and remodeled products. And three, they exhibited superior organizational learning in achieving continuing progress throughout their operations in raising productivity, in improving quality, and in resolving other kinds of issues that arise in manufacturing.

In this chapter, we will examine the organizational capability implicit in those three features and the mechanisms by which the Japanese manufacturers translated that capability into deep competitiveness. We will see that the internationally successful Japanese manufacturers possessed thoroughgoing and difficult-to-emulate routines for communicating and storing design information in the manufacturing workplace and in the product development workplace. We will discover impressive strengths in creating and in transferring design information efficiently, rapidly, and accurately. And we will find the best example of the organizational capability in question at that paragon of modern manufacturing, Toyota.

FIGURE 3-1

Design Information Transfer Time in Gross Working Hours and in Gross Production Lead Time

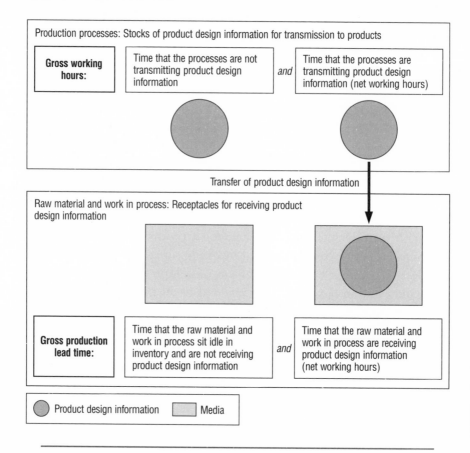

Product design information   Media

---

1. The Parameters of Deep Competitiveness in Manufacturing and in Product Development

Manufacturing productivity

Here is a useful definition of manufacturing productivity in light of our understanding of products as media infused with information: the efficiency of people and equipment in production processes in transmitting accumulated design information to raw materials and to work in process.

We speak of the efficiency of people in transmitting design information as labor productivity. The corresponding indicator for equipment is capital productivity.

Net working time is thus the time during which a production process is transmitting design information to the product media (fig. 3-1, upper half). In other words, labor time is a combination of productive time, when information is being transmitted, and unproductive time, when information is stagnant. We ordinarily calculate labor productivity in a manufacturing process as unit production per hours worked. But we can calculate it more usefully as net working speed (unit production per hour of information transfer) times the net labor rate (hours of actual information transfer per hours of labor).

Efforts to raise labor productivity in U.S. manufacturing in the 20th century focused on maximizing net working speed. Manufacturers typically strived to shorten cycle times by assigning workers to single tasks and by deploying highly specialized equipment. Japanese manufacturers focused on the other element of productivity: the net labor rate. They strived to raise that rate by equipping workers with multiple skills and by putting the multiskilled employees in charge of multiple tasks. The success of the Toyota Production System suggests that the latter approach was more effective in increasing productivity.

Manufacturing lead times

A distinction between net time and gross time is also useful in focusing efforts effectively on shortening manufacturing lead times. That is, we can do better than simply measure the time from when raw material or work in process enters a process to when it leaves the process. We can recognize that manufacturing lead time is a combination of productive time—when the material is receiving design information—and unproductive time—when it is not (fig. 3-1, lower half). Manufacturers can shorten lead times by finding ways to transfer information more quickly during the productive time—the net working time—and by finding ways to reduce the unproductive time, when material is sitting idle in a warehouse or elsewhere.

Successful Japanese manufacturers, led by Toyota, have focused mainly on reducing unproductive time in their efforts to shorten lead time.

They have been especially aggressive in keeping material items out of the warehouse and in the production flow. Toyota's just-in-time production synchronizes the processing of small lots throughout the manufacturing sequence. That maintains a nearly continuous transfer of design information to the material and thereby converts the material swiftly into finished products.

Manufacturing quality

Design information can deteriorate en route to finished products like a phrase gets distorted in the game Gossip (a party game where people convey a phrase by whispering it to one another in turn). Achieving high manufacturing quality is a matter of preventing that deterioration and transferring the design information accurately to the finished products.

The path of design information passes from the creation of product designs through process design and engineering and into the finished products via processing in manufacturing. U.S. and European automakers traditionally relied on inspections at the end of the manufacturing sequence to ensure quality conformance—to ensure that the finished products conformed closely to the design information. The Japanese automakers have achieved higher quality by concentrating instead on building quality into the manufacturing processes.

Japan's automakers have trained and equipped workers to monitor the quality of their work while processing material, and they have designed equipment and systems to detect irregularities immediately and to stop when problems occur to prevent defective items from progressing into the following process. Here again, the Japanese have improved their manufacturing performance by investing people and equipment with the capacity for handling multiple tasks—inspection, as well as processing.

Productivity, lead time, and quality in product development

The deep competitiveness of productivity, lead time, and quality in manufacturing is thus a matter of how efficiently, swiftly, and accurately manufacturers transfer design information to products. In product development, it is a matter of how efficiently, swiftly, and accurately they create information for the purpose of problem solving.

Manufacturers draw on their knowledge and understanding of markets and available technologies in striving to plan and design original products. They also draw on their market and technological knowledge and understanding in equipping their manufacturing processes with the equipment, tools, manuals, and other resources necessary for commercial production.

All of this activity is essentially an attempt to identify customer needs and wants and to bring technology to bear in fulfilling those needs and wants. A development project for a new product is thus a series of exercises in problem solving. The sequence of creating a product concept, a basic design, and a detailed design for a new vehicle, for example, entails literally thousands of problem-solving cycles.

2. Distinctive Elements of Japanese Production Systems

Several distinctive elements characterize the organizational capability that underlay the strengths that Toyota and other Japanese manufacturers asserted in the 1980s and 1990s. Here is a highly arbitrary sampling of some especially important features of Japanese product development, manufacturing, and purchasing.

Product development

Personifying Japanese product development was the product manager. At Toyota and to a lesser extent at other Japanese automakers, the product manager—"chief engineer" at Toyota—asserted near-absolute control over product-development projects. His authority cut across functional lines of command. For example, automotive engineers responsible for such functional components as the body, engine, and suspension worked under general managers responsible for their functional specialties. But when they participated in a vehicle-development project, they answered to the product manager responsible for that project.

Another characteristic element of Japanese product development was simultaneous engineering. The manufacturers developed systems simultaneously that their U.S. and European counterparts had traditionally developed in sequence. And they secured the participation of parts and materials suppliers in the early stages of development projects under the name design-in. The combination of simultaneous engineering and design-in shortened lead times greatly in product development. Also contributing to shortening lead times was an astonishing attention to speed and quality in fabricating prototypes, molds, dies, and jigs.

Yet another characteristic of Japanese product development was the small size of the teams assigned to each phase of activity. Training and deploying multiskilled engineers and technicians gave the teams a versatility and flexibility that would have been impossible with larger teams of narrowly trained specialists.

Manufacturing

In manufacturing, Japanese manufacturers developed a vast repertoire of tools for maximizing productivity, for ensuring quality, and for minimizing lead times. Best known is Toyota's just-in-time approach to production management. Just-in-time management ensures that each process produces only what is needed by the following process, only in the amount needed, and only when it is needed. Also famous are the *kanban* information cards (now giving way to digital markers) that Toyota attached to work in process to enforce just-in-time flows.

Less well known but equally important is Toyota's *jidoka*, a play on the Japanese words for automation and for human (intelligent) work. *Jidoka* included measures for equipping machines to detect irregularities and to stop immediately when they occurred. As we have seen, that prevented defective items from proceeding to the following process and avoided the waste of consuming resources in producing defective output. Stopping immediately when irregularities occurred yielded the additional virtue of illuminating the causes of the problems.

In the same spirit, Toyota's line-stop mechanisms enabled anyone on the production line to stop the line in their process. Pulling a line-stop cord would light a lamp to call attention to a problem and summon a supervisor. The line didn't actually stop until it reached a position where each person had completed a full cycle of work. If the supervisor could resolve the problem before the line reached that point, he or she would pull on the line-stop cord to cancel the stop and keep the line moving. Otherwise, the line would stop at the prescribed position until the problem was resolved.

Toyota and other Japanese manufacturers overturned a traditional tenet of mass production with their leveling of production. Leveling means distributing the production of different models and kinds of parts evenly over the day or week. Manufacturers traditionally had endeavored to maximize mass-production efficiencies by producing one item at a time and in large batches. That resulted in large inventories, which tied up financial resources, required vast storage space and extensive handling, and could burden the manufacturer with unsold goods if demand shifted. Leveling helped minimize inventories, and it allowed for deploying resources optimally throughout the production sequence. That is because leveling allowed for deploying production capacity to serve the average, rather than the peak, level of demand.

Japanese manufacturers famously mobilized their entire production teams in the kaizen pursuit of continuing improvements. They developed innovative production layouts that maximized efficiency in the flow of work. And they devised startlingly economical ways to automate work.

Purchasing

The Japanese revolution in manufacturing transformed purchasing practices. Japan's manufacturers eschewed internal integration and turned to suppliers—some independent, some closely affiliated—for a large portion of their parts and materials. They developed supplier hierarchies in which a limited number of large, first-tier suppliers delivered subassemblies directly to the assembly manufacturers. Second-tier suppliers provided their output to the assembly manufacturers through the first-tier suppliers, third-tier suppliers through the second-tier suppliers, and so on.

Japanese assembly manufacturers provided trusted suppliers with mere outlines of needed parts and relied on the suppliers to create detailed designs. They evaluated suppliers partly on the basis of capabilities in generating original designs and in undertaking kaizen. That promoted continuing competition among the suppliers in building those capabilities. The assembly manufacturers expected suppliers to achieve continuing cost reductions and to lower their prices in step with those reductions. Periodic inspections of suppliers' plants by representatives of the assembly manufacturers were a matter of course. And the suppliers received and welcomed technical guidance from their customer manufacturers.

The common thread: product design information

Space does not allow us to indulge in a comprehensive review of the characteristics of Japanese product development, manufacturing, and purchasing. The examples cited demonstrate, however, that successful Japanese manufacturers in the 1980s and 1990s differed fundamentally from traditional mass producers in North America and Europe. Note that the examples cited are highly interrelated. They all form part of integrated systems for strengthening the deep competitiveness of high productivity, short lead time, high conformance quality, and high design quality. And that deep competitiveness expresses itself in the surface competitiveness—customer appeal—of persuasive price, compelling content, and ready availability.

Each of the elements of deep competitiveness cited above is the result of a well-established organizational routine. Only when the multifarious organizational routines come together in organic linkage do they increase a manufacturer's competitiveness in product development, manufacturing, or purchasing. To analyze the management and interplay of those routines, we need to find the common thread by which they interact. That common thread is product design information.

We can portray organizational capability at manufacturers accurately by elucidating how each routine figures in the process of creating and transferring design information. Our portrait here will be of organizational capability at automakers. We will examine the organizational capability that Toyota and other Japanese automakers asserted in the last 25 years or so of the 20th century. Our examination will focus on product development, on manufacturing, on kaizen continuous improvement in the production workplace, and on parts purchasing.

Optimizing design information in product development

The Japanese automakers' success in shortening lead time in product development has raised their accuracy in targeting demand. Every development project is essentially an educated guess about future trends in demand. The less time required to move a product concept from the drawing board to the showroom, the more accurate that guess is likely to be.

Raising productivity in product development, meanwhile, has enabled the Japanese automakers to conduct development projects. Higher productivity increases the number of projects that are possible with the same allocation of funding, engineers, material, and other resources. That has enabled the Japanese automakers to serve a greater range of demand and to address the growing diversity of demand more comprehensively.

The Japanese automakers have also increased the effectiveness of their development projects by using generally small project teams. Assigning broad-ranging responsibilities to the team members gives each member a broad perspective on the project. That improves communication and efficiency hugely in conducting product development.

Further increasing the effectiveness of product development at some Japanese automakers is the immense power invested in the product managers. Those managers wield authority over the entire sequence, from developing product concepts through translating the concepts into detailed designs to putting them into mass production. They are as proficient in the language of consumers and of salespeople as they are in the technical lingo of engineers and designers. Curiously, the other characteristics of Japanese product development discussed here have long been common to all Japanese automakers, but the all-powerful product manager is unique to Toyota.

Also characterizing product development at the Japanese automakers is close communication between the product designers and their counterparts in production engineering, on the plant floor, and elsewhere in their companies. That communication begins in the earliest stages of conceiving vehicle models. The participation of production people in those stages helps the development team anticipate potential issues in mass production and allows for shaping designs to facilitate efficient assembly. It also allows for starting work on production equipment and plant layouts for manufacturing the new vehicle models while the models are still in development. That is one aspect of the simultaneous engineering mentioned earlier.

All of the characteristic features of product development at the Japanese automakers contribute to speed and accuracy—conformance to marketplace demand—in creating design information. Figure 3-2 presents a schematic diagram of the interaction of those features.

FIGURE 3-2

Organizational Capability in Integrated Product Development

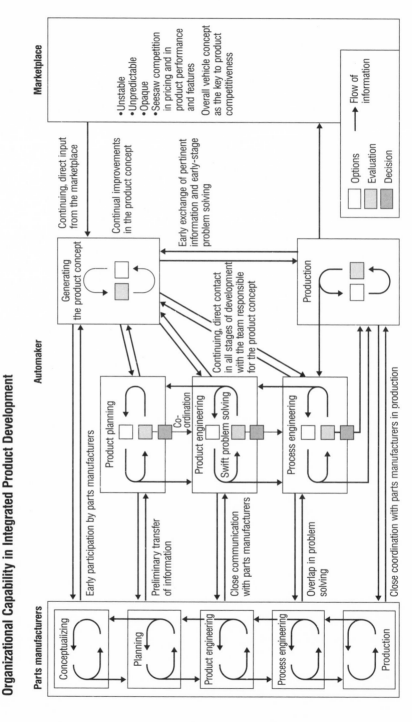

Raising the density of information transferal in manufacturing

Toyota and other Japanese manufacturers have built integrated manufacturing systems in which (1) the percentage of time that raw material and work in progress spend actually receiving value-added information is high, (2) the percentage of operating and working time that equipment and workers spend actually transferring value-added information to raw material and to work in progress is high, and (3) the accuracy of the information transfer is high. These three strengths, as we have seen, are manifest in short lead times, high productivity, and high quality. Figure 3-3 presents a schematic diagram of Toyota's format for ensuring a robust and accurate flow of information in manufacturing.

Energizing the system are continuing kaizen improvements in production processes and in work procedures. The main emphasis in improving process design and layout is on reducing the time that raw material and work in progress are not actually receiving value-added information. And the main emphasis in improving work procedures is on reducing the time that equipment and workers are not actually transmitting value-added information to the raw material and work in progress. Eliminating waste—*muda* in Japanese—is the central dynamic of the Toyota Production System. The people at Toyota are especially alert to the waste of stagnant information or stagnant material in the production flow.

Kaizen improvements in production processes can occasion temporary declines in the percentage of operating and working time that equipment and workers spend transmitting information. Follow-up kaizen improvements in work procedures become necessary to match the increased efficiency engendered by the kaizen in process design and layout.

Achieving further increases in net information transfer time can be extremely difficult on well-established, well-managed production lines. Synchronizing the pace of activity in upstream and downstream processes is essential. Also useful is leveling production—distributing the production of different items evenly over the shift, day, week, or any other time frame. Leveling production helps increase the density of manufacturing activity in regard to information transfer, but it entails frequent changeovers of tools and dies. Achieving the benefits of leveled production thus hinges on continuing improvements in shortening the changeover times.

FIGURE 3-3

Organizational Capability in the Toyota Production System: Productivity and Lead Time

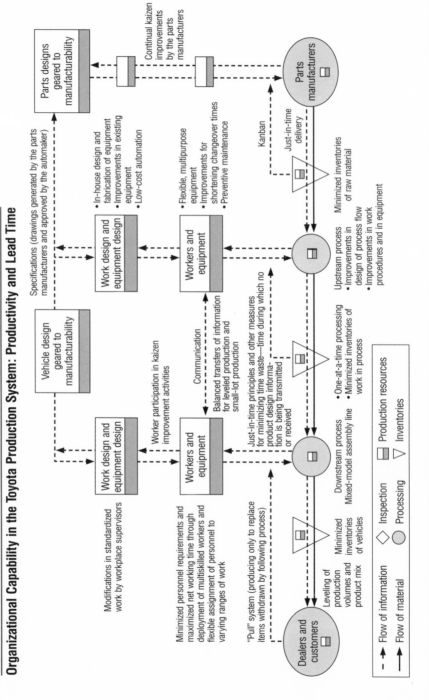

Also useful in increasing net information transfer time is the characteristically Japanese emphasis on versatility—on cultivating multiskilled workers, on assigning workers to handle multiple tasks, and on designing processes to accommodate a broad range of work. The versatility of the workers and processes at the Japanese automakers enables the automakers to respond flexibly and cost-effectively to changes in production volumes. An automaker can respond to a decline in demand for a model by reducing the number of people on the production line and broadening the range of tasks handled by each person. When demand for a model increases, the automaker can deploy more people on the line and narrow the range of tasks handled by each individual.

That versatility—human and mechanical—is the result of investing workers and equipment with more information than they require for any individual task. Amassing the extra information raises costs, most notably in the increased worker training that it demands, but the resultant increase in the density of information transferal in manufacturing more than justifies the expense.

Maintaining the integrity of the information

Consistently high quality is the great precondition for all activity at the Japanese automakers. From the automakers' perspective, high productivity and short lead times are only meaningful if accompanied by near-absolute quality. We have seen that improvements in productivity and in lead time commonly begin on the receiving side of the design information transfers. Initial improvements in the design and layout of the production processes occasion follow-up improvements in work procedures.

In contrast, primary responsibility for improving quality assurance—that is, for increasing accuracy in transferring design information—resides on the transmission side of the information transfers. Japanese vehicle plants abound in features for ensuring the integrity of the design information that workers and equipment transmit to raw material and to work in progress. The Japanese automakers characterize those features as a means of building quality into the production processes.

Adhering to standardized work procedures, conducting thorough and continuing training, and performing preventive maintenance all help preserve the integrity of the design information supplied to production

FIGURE 3-4

Organizational Capability in the Toyota Production System: Manufacturing Quality (Quality of Conformance)

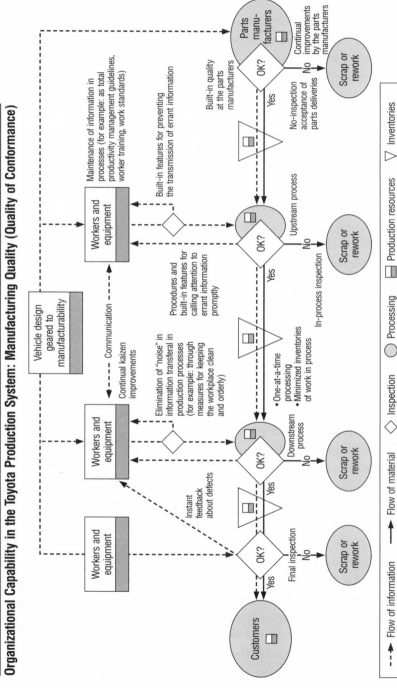

processes. Inside the processes, fail-safe features for preventing malfunctions help ensure the accurate transferal of design information. The characteristically Japanese devotion to the S's of *seiri* (specifying the correct places for tools and other items in the workplace); *seiton* (being neat and always returning items to their proper places); and *seiso* (keeping the workplace clean) helps prevent "noise" during information transferal in the production processes. Meanwhile, the Japanese automakers minimize the impact of any glitches by making workers responsible for monitoring the quality of their output, by providing equipment with automatic inspection functions, by maintaining minimal inventories of semifinished goods, and by processing items one at a time or in the smallest-possible batches (fig. 3-4).

Kaizen improvements as problem-solving cycles

The capacity for continuing kaizen improvements is an indispensable facet of the Japanese automakers' organizational capability. Kaizen unfold as problem-solving cycles, and we can identify five defining characteristics of those cycles (fig. 3-5):
1. Enforced detection of problems
2. Devolution of authority to the workplace
3. Standardized tools
4. Swift action
5. Cumulative improvements

Enforced detection of problems
Features for forcibly bringing problems to people's attention are in evidence throughout the plants of the Japanese automakers. Enforced detection means making the status of work visible to everyone and calling attention to problems immediately when they occur. Just-in-time production links processes integrally, so even a brief stoppage in any process is instantly apparent to people in the preceding and following processes. Toyota's *jidoka*, as we have seen, enables people and equips machines with the means of calling attention to problems and of stopping the line, if necessary, to resolve the problems. The Japanese automakers' dedication to keeping the workplace orderly, neat, and clean also helps ensure that problems become visible immediately.

FIGURE 3-5

An Example of Problem-Solving and Kaizen Cycles in an Integrated Production System

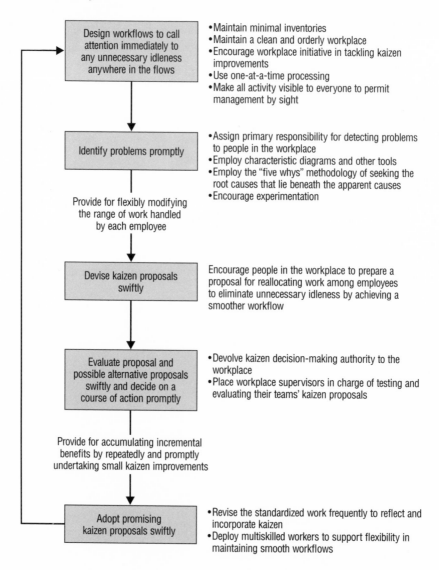

Design workflows to call attention immediately to any unnecessary idleness anywhere in the flows

- Maintain minimal inventories
- Maintain a clean and orderly workplace
- Encourage workplace initiative in tackling kaizen improvements
- Use one-at-a-time processing
- Make all activity visible to everyone to permit management by sight

Identify problems promptly

- Assign primary responsibility for detecting problems to people in the workplace
- Employ characteristic diagrams and other tools
- Employ the "five whys" methodology of seeking the root causes that lie beneath the apparent causes
- Encourage experimentation

Provide for flexibly modifying the range of work handled by each employee

Devise kaizen proposals swiftly

Encourage people in the workplace to prepare a proposal for reallocating work among employees to eliminate unnecessary idleness by achieving a smoother workflow

Evaluate proposal and possible alternative proposals swiftly and decide on a course of action promptly

- Devolve kaizen decision-making authority to the workplace
- Place workplace supervisors in charge of testing and evaluating their teams' kaizen proposals

Provide for accumulating incremental benefits by repeatedly and promptly undertaking small kaizen improvements

Adopt promising kaizen proposals swiftly

- Revise the standardized work frequently to reflect and incorporate kaizen
- Deploy multiskilled workers to support flexibility in maintaining smooth workflows

Devolution of authority to the workplace

When problems arise at Japanese vehicle plants, problem-solving cycles begin turning promptly in the workplace. People in the workplaces where the problems occur take responsibility for resolving the problems. They are, after all, the people most familiar with the situation. Tapping their accumulated knowledge and understanding is the most effective way to solve most problems.

The line workers and their supervisors analyze the problems and devise solutions. They might seek the cooperation of equipment maintenance people, of members of specialized kaizen teams, or of production engineers. The group leaders responsible for the plant worksites have the power to authorize changes in standardized work and in equipment.

Note that the workers and their supervisors initially try to resolve problems by modifying the work procedures. Only when modifications in procedures prove insufficient to resolve the problems do they resort to modifications in equipment. The idea is to resolve problems as inexpensively and as quickly as possible.

Standardized tools

Just as the Japanese automakers employ standardized work procedures for production tasks, they also employ highly standardized procedures for problem solving. Identifying and solving problems, in other words, are part of the repertoire of routines that defines activity at each vehicle plant. The automakers teach the kaizen routines to everyone in their plants. People take pride in demonstrating their growing ability to detect possible problems and to take part in devising solutions.

Swift action

The cardinal rule in kaizen is to try *something* immediately when problems become apparent. Rather than entrusting an issue to a committee for deliberation, the preferred approach is to secure the approval of the group leader and to make a change promptly. Workers modify their work procedures under the supervision of their group leader and monitor the results. If a change fails to resolve the problem, they try something else and keep trying until the problem is solved.

Significant changes in the standardized work procedures require written proposals, review, and approval. But workers and their supervisors commonly experiment with measures for solving problems before submitting formal proposals. The written proposals thus tend to carry the persuasiveness of tried and proved solutions.

Cumulative improvements

Standardized work—carefully taught and scrupulously observed at the Japanese automakers—is the vessel for retaining the advances of kaizen improvements. Only when workers perform tasks consistently in accordance with the prescribed procedures do companies have a basis for improving work. Conversely, adhering to the standardized work invests each worker's performance with improvements accumulated over decades of problem solving. From the standpoint of capability-building competition, it ensures that improvements made today will generate continuing, cumulative contributions to companies' competitiveness.

Empowering workers to take the initiative in identifying and resolving problems has struck some observers as a reversal of Taylorism—the top-down "scientific management" pioneered in the early 20th century by the American Fredrick Taylor. Japanese standardized work and kaizen, however, are every bit as rigorous as Taylorism in requiring adherence to specified work procedures. We should think of them not as a rejection of Taylorism but as the democratization of Taylor's principles.

Managing supplier relationships effectively

The vehicle manufacturers' networks of suppliers of parts and services are extensions of their internal capabilities in product development and manufacturing. The ability to steer suppliers toward achieving high productivity, short lead time, and high quality is an indispensable facet of organizational capability. The automakers' relationships with suppliers center on negotiating supply contracts for individual components, on selecting suppliers, and on working out the division of labor. Japan's automakers have maximized their organizational capability in purchasing by building long-term relationships with suppliers, by promoting competition among small groups of core suppliers, and by obtaining parts through comprehensive purchasing agreements.

Long-term relationships occasion a vast sharing of information, which raises efficiency immensely in product development and in manufacturing.

That includes raising efficiency in solving problems that are not necessarily attributable entirely to one company or the other. Efficiency also benefits immensely from the bonds of trust that underlie the long-term relationships and that grow stronger as those relationships develop. A classic example is the way that the Japanese vehicle manufacturers dispense with the acceptance inspections of parts delivered by trusted suppliers.

The Japanese automakers' predilection for building long-term relationships has resulted in closely knit groups of core suppliers. Each automaker tends to solicit tenders for crucial parts from two or three suppliers among "the usual suspects." The narrow range of sourcing suggests the possibility of oligopolistic manipulation by the suppliers. In fact, the opposite is the case. Familiarity, at least in Japan, breeds competition. Transparency in cost competitiveness foments intense price competition, and the suppliers strive to differentiate their offerings advantageously by asserting an edge in other phases of competitiveness. The vitality of the Japanese automobile industry over the past half-century is testimony to the ferocity of that competition.

Further underpinning the contribution of supplier networks to the Japanese automakers' deep competitiveness are the comprehensive supply arrangements that they permit. Japan's vehicle manufacturers expect core suppliers to undertake responsibility for developing subassemblies based on broad performance criteria, for conducting performance evaluations of the subassemblies in the context of vehicle systems, and for ensuring the quality of parts supplied by second- and third-tier suppliers. Interaction with a limited number of core suppliers thus leverages the automakers' organizational capability across a tremendous range of manufacturing.

4 The History of Capability Building in the Automobile Industry

Two questions arise about the organizational capability and deep competitiveness that the Japanese automakers built in the latter half of the 20th century. One, how did the Japanese automakers steal a march on the U.S. and European automakers in building that capability and that competitiveness? And two, why didn't the Americans and the Europeans notice what was going on at the time?

What we discover about the world-beating production systems built by the Japanese automakers is surprising. We find that the systems emerged as the unplanned and unexpected result of countless individual and seemingly unrelated innovations, improvements, and initiatives. The Japanese automakers, in other words, did not set out to create new kinds of production systems. Rather, their systems emerged through piecemeal, ad hoc measures for addressing needs and issues that arose in their business and operations.

The Japanese had no idea—in any systematic, big-picture sense—what they were doing. And if they themselves were unaware of what they were doing, the U.S. and European automakers could hardly have noticed what was happening. Nor could the Americans or Europeans have easily emulated the Japanese's capability building even had they noticed what was happening.

1. The Dawn of an Industry

American dominance

Inventive Japanese began making gasoline-powered vehicles around 1910. A lot of the inventors, as in other nations, had honed their mechanical skills on horse-drawn wagons or bicycles. None of them built lasting businesses in vehicle manufacturing.

Mass production of automobiles didn't get under way in Japan until the 1920s. The nation's first large vehicle plants were Ford- and General Motors–owned operations that assembled sets of parts imported from the United States. They produced mainly trucks, and they commanded fully 90% of the Japanese market by the early 1930s. The industry, however, was a mere shadow of its U.S. counterpart. Annual vehicle production in Japan never reached more than 50,000 vehicles in the prewar years, whereas U.S. plants were turning out some 5 million vehicles a year.

Toyota and Nissan before the war

Japan's handful of native vehicle manufacturers had eked out a protected subsistence largely by filling government orders for military trucks. In 1936, the Japanese government turned the entire industry over to domestic manufacturers. It enacted draconian legislation that essentially forced the Americans out of the Japanese market. Accompanying that legislation were permits for Nissan and Toyota to begin producing trucks for the military. Toyoda Automatic Loom Works was building prototype vehicles in a skunk works project that it later incorporated as the forebear of Toyota Motor Corporation. (The *d* in the family name, Toyoda, became the more-common and presumably more-marketable *t* for purposes of automobile branding.)

Nissan's and Toyota's trucks contained a lot of design information gleaned from U.S. vehicles. The two companies employed notably different approaches, however, in the ways they adopted that information.

Toyota reverse engineered—that is, disassembled, analyzed, and copied—Chevrolet and Ford vehicles. It modified parts designs for its purposes and incorporated them in prototype trucks and sedans. Toyota also used numerous replacement parts from U.S. automakers in its early models. But Toyota engineers insisted on developing the overall vehicle designs on their own.

Nissan, in contrast, obtained a lot of its product and production technology lock, stock, and barrel. It purchased detailed drawings and production equipment for trucks from the U.S. automaker Graham-Paige, which had withdrawn from the truck business.

The best-effort results of both approaches were trucks that were conspicuously inferior to their U.S. counterparts in durability and in reliability. Nissan and Toyota both received continuing criticism from the military and from their other principal customers. Productivity, too, was far lower at the Japanese vehicle manufacturers than at the U.S. automakers. Toyota's productivity was only 10% of Ford's from the 1930s to the mid-1940s, according to Toyota sources.

An interesting historical footnote is the story of the three-wheeled trucks that became ubiquitous in Japan in the 1930s. Those vehicles were mechanically simpler than four-wheeled trucks, and they required fewer parts. A dozen or more Japanese companies produced the three-wheeled trucks, some until the 1960s, and the distinctive-looking vehicles remained highly visible around Japanese workshops and farms into the 1980s. They were a classic demonstration of ingenuity in adapting technology to the circumstances of manufacturers and customers.

Kiichiro's big idea

The automotive skunk works project at Toyoda Automatic Loom Works got under way around 1931. Heading the project was Kiichiro (kee-ee-chee-roh) Toyoda (1894–1952), the eldest son of Toyota Group founder Sakichi Toyoda (1867–1930). Kiichiro recognized the superiority of U.S. products and production technology, but he also recognized that adaptations would be necessary to make automobiles and automobile manufacturing viable in Japan. Modifications in product specifications would be necessary, for example, to accommodate Japan's largely unpaved and undeveloped roadways, and modifications in production methods would be necessary to achieve viable productivity in Japan's still-tiny market for motor vehicles.

For Kiichiro, the thought of taking on some of the world's biggest and most powerful companies appears to have been motivating rather than discouraging. His skunk works team started with research and development work on engines and gradually began fabricating prototype vehicles. He purchased U.S. vehicles, disassembled them, and made meticulous sketches of the parts. Using numerous genuine replacement parts for Chevrolet and Ford vehicles, Kiichiro's team crafted prototypes for the A1 passenger car and the G1 truck.

Toyoda Automatic Loom Works spun off its fledgling automotive venture as Toyota Motor Co., Ltd., in 1937. Bold plans for establishing an internationally competitive enterprise were part of the company's founding vision. "We will achieve costs with production volumes of 20,000 or 30,000 vehicles a year," declared Kiichiro, "that are competitive with U.S. costs in producing hundreds of thousands of vehicles a year."

Toyota Motor opened its first dedicated vehicle plant in 1938. The plant was in Koromo, a town outside Nagoya that has since changed its name to Toyota City. To fulfill his vision, Kiichiro set about adapting U.S. mass-production methods to small-volume production. The U.S. automakers used large numbers of stamping machines, for example, which entailed huge investment. Kiichiro minimized fixed costs by using hand tools instead for some of the stamping work. He exhibited the characteristic Toyota preoccupation with flexibility in deploying machine tools that accommodated changing specifications.

The Koromo Plant never attained production capacity of more than 2,000 vehicles a month during the prewar years. War brought demand for military trucks, but no significant advances in production methods occurred during the war years. Not until the postwar years would Toyota achieve its epochal breakthroughs in lean manufacturing.

2. Rethinking Production

Starting over

After the war, Japan's automakers scraped together whatever production equipment was undamaged or at least still serviceable and resumed making trucks. Their total output, however, had reached only 30,000 vehicles by 1950—well below the prewar peak. Vehicle production in Japan gradually climbed above the prewar level, but the volume was still an unimpressive 70,000 units in 1955.

Japanese automakers began investing in production equipment. Interesting things happened at Toyota, though, that had little to do with capital spending. Productivity in Toyota's production processes surged some 10-fold. The company, barely solvent, had not made any dramatic investment in new equipment. Nor had its production volume increased anywhere near enough to account for that kind of rise in productivity.

We see in retrospect that several factors figured in Toyota's surging productivity. People at the company had done their homework. They had learned the principles of the Ford system and had adopted pertinent elements of that system throughout their operations. They had also mastered the principles of Fredrick Taylor's scientific management. In addition, they had started applying just-in-time principles, which had begun to take shape at Toyota before the war.

Let us bear in mind, however, that even at Toyota people were, in effect, improvising. They were studying hard and achieving important advances in productivity, quality, and lead time. But they lacked a comprehensive blueprint for their diverse and wide-ranging efforts. Kiichiro's dream of achieving international competitiveness presumably inspired the progress. But the author finds no evidence of any conscious or concrete "grand design" behind the improvements and advances that laid the foundation for the Toyota Production System.

Postwar rebuilding segued into economic boom, and vehicle production burgeoned. Japan's automakers were churning out some 500,000 vehicles a year by 1960 and 10 times that many by 1970. By 1980, annual vehicle production in Japan had reached about 11 million units.

Integrated vehicle plants capable of turning out 200,000-some vehicles a year—mainly passenger cars—multiplied on the Japanese landscape in the 1960s. Mechanization and automation proceeded on a massive scale in machining and forming work. Several companies that had produced three-wheeled trucks in the 1950s withdrew from vehicle manufacturing, and the industry had coalesced into an 11-company lineup—including a couple of companies that specialized in trucks and buses—by the mid-1960s. Some of those companies have since become subsidiaries of other Japanese automakers or of foreign automakers, and some have concluded other kinds of partnerships, sometimes accompanied by significant equity investments. The basic lineup, however, has proved remarkably resilient.

Japan's automakers have a broad range of industrial pedigrees. Toyota and Suzuki are the offspring of manufacturers of textiles and textile-manufacturing equipment. Subaru emerged from the aircraft operations at Fuji Heavy Industries. Also an offshoot of aircraft manufacturing was Prince, a vehicle manufacturer absorbed by Nissan in the mid-1960s. Mitsubishi Motors and the truck and bus maker Mitsubishi Fuso originated in the shipbuilding operations at Mitsubishi Heavy Industries. Daihatsu and Mazda are former manufacturers of three-wheeled trucks.

Honda produced motorcycles and motor scooters before it began making automobiles, as did Suzuki. Nissan has a complex pedigree, but its forebears include a company established in the early 20th century expressly to produce motorcars. Isuzu, too, was a vehicle manufacturer from the beginning.

Domestic demand drove the growth of Japan's automobile industry up to the 1960s, but exports became the industry's chief driver in the 1970s. Japan's vehicle exports, only about 40,000 units in 1960, had multiplied to around 1 million units by 1970 and to some 6 million by 1980. They peaked at 6.7 million in 1985, the year of the Plaza Accord. That accord was an agreement among the United States, Japan, Germany, the United Kingdom, and France to devalue the U.S. dollar relative to the yen and to the mark.

The strengthened yen, along with trade frictions, prompted the Japanese automakers to expand their vehicle production outside Japan, and their exports declined sharply. By the mid-1990s, vehicle exports from Japan had declined to about 4 million units a year. They remained around that level for the rest of the decade, though they resumed rising after the turn of the century. Meanwhile, the Japanese automakers' vehicle production outside Japan had reached nearly 7 million units annually by the year 2000.

Kiichiro redux

"Catch up with the United States in productivity within three years." Kiichiro Toyoda issued that brash directive in autumn 1945. Toyota and other Japanese automakers were using what remained of their plant and equipment to gradually resume vehicle—truck—production. Shortages of funding and hardware, however, sorely crimped their efforts. And Kiichiro recognized that attaining viability in automobile manufacturing would require a quantum leap in productivity.

The bold notion of leaping to the U.S. level of productivity in just three years proved unrealistic. But Toyota did in fact achieve a stunning increase in efficiency. The man known as the father of the Toyota Production System, Taiichi (tie-ee-chee) Ohno (1912–1990), described that increase in an interview attended by the author. According to Ohno, productivity in Toyota's principal machine shops rose some 10-fold in the first decade after World War II. Ohno toured the engine factory of a U.S. automaker in 1956, and Toyota's productivity in terms of unit output per worker was already higher than what he witnessed there.

Japan's automakers needed to find ways to raise productivity without relying on extensive capital spending and without benefiting from significant economies of scale. They therefore sought ways to raise their productivity mainly through improvements in methods—improvements that did not require cash investment. They standardized work, leveled production, rationalized plant layouts, and equipped their workers with multiskilled capabilities to allow for handling multiple tasks. They leveraged their scarce funding for capital spending by investing it in low-cost, multipurpose jigs and other items that accommodated changing product specifications inexpensively.

Impressive improvements in productivity were under way on the floor of the vehicle assembly plants in the late 1940s. But overall production control remained primitive. The parts suppliers would produce their parts in large batches and bring them in whenever the batches were complete. The automakers never knew when they would be able to go to work on assembling their vehicles. Obtaining the parts for a month's allotment of vehicles tended to take three weeks or so. The automakers would then spend the last 10 days of the month frantically assembling the vehicles.

Irregular parts delivery thus prevented the automakers from leveling production as much as they could have. It obliged them to maintain enough people and equipment to handle the production rush at the end of each month. Distributing the parts deliveries evenly and reliably through the month would enable the automakers to make do with one-third as many workers. That is exactly what Ohno accomplished with just-in-time production management. He recalled in the interview cited that he had used just in time to level production in Toyota machine shops by 1950.

Another obstacle to productivity gains was the tendency to group machine tools by kind: drilling machines here, lathes over there, milling machines elsewhere. Toyota and other Japanese automakers redeployed their machine tools individually in the production sequence for each product. That initially entailed an increase in the overall number of machine tools and a decline in overall capacity utilization rates. But it reduced inventories dramatically. And in conjunction with multiskill training for equipping workers to handle multiple tasks and even multiple machines, it reduced labor requirements dramatically. Ohno described how he reduced the labor requirements in important machining processes from the prewar three or four workers per machine to one worker per machine and gradually to one worker for multiple machines.

Standardized work, meanwhile, took control of the production flow out of the subjective hands of craftsman-like foremen and placed it in the objective grasp of modern management. In the immediate postwar years, Toyota's machine shops were completely under the sway of the foremen. Those quasi-autonomous artisans retained total responsibility for the volume and quality of the output of the teams under their authority. The white-collar managers nominally responsible for the machine shops kept their distance. They could do nothing directly to resolve problems and could only make excuses for the chronic delays in production.

Ohno and his subordinates prepared manuals that detailed standardized work for all activity in the machine shops, and they posted the standardized work charts in plain view at every workstation. In addition, Ohno declared that making continual improvements in the standardized work was everyone's responsibility. Any standardized work left unchanged for a month, he declared, would mean that people weren't doing their jobs. Standardized work encountered initial resistance from the foremen, but it soon took hold throughout Toyota's machine shops.

3. Laying a Foundation for Passenger Car Manufacturing

Design

An interesting historical aspect of Japan's automobile industry is the central position of truck production in the industry's development. Vehicle production in early-postwar Japan consisted almost exclusively of trucks. Not until the late 1960s—when Japanese vehicle ownership surged—did passenger cars outnumber trucks and other commercial vehicles in Japan's vehicle output.

Japanese product development in passenger cars was initially a matter of mounting passenger car bodies on truck chassis. That approach entailed shortcomings in regard to comfort and performance. But it offered important advantages in regard to employing established product and production technology, leveraging investment, and fostering economies of scale.

Some of Japan's automakers—notably Hino, Isuzu, and Nissan—moved in the 1950s to secure modern passenger car technology from abroad. They did that by producing cars under license from foreign—mainly European—automakers. That licensed production of passenger cars continued until the early 1960s, but the production volumes were small: only between 2,000 and 4,000 cars a year per automaker. In the late 1950s, Japanese auto parts makers began licensing technology extensively from overseas manufacturers, mainly in the United States.

Toyota's crisis

Japan's government adopted a policy of financial retrenchment in 1948 and 1949, and the resultant slump in demand for vehicles was nearly disastrous for Toyota. Burdened with crushing inventories of unsold vehicles, management resorted to drastic measures to cope with the crisis. Toyota secured emergency loans from financial institutions, spun off its sales arm, and dismissed about 2,000 workers, which led to an acrimonious labor dispute in 1950. Chastened by the ordeal, management and labor at Toyota united in a joint commitment to ensuring stable employment. They resolved to avoid producing any more vehicles than they could be certain of selling. Note that their emphasis on linking production to actual demand echoed and reinforced a basic tenet of just-in-time production.

The outbreak of the Korean War kindled a recovery in vehicle demand, led by orders from the U.S. military for trucks. Toyota lacked the financial latitude to invest in new plant and equipment, and the new labor-management understanding precluded hiring more workers than management could be sure of retaining over the long term. So the people at Toyota found ways to raise productivity and thereby meet the increased demand while using their old plant and equipment and without expanding the company's payroll. That response established a pattern that would continue to characterize management policy at Toyota: cope with upturns in demand by finding ways to increase output without adding equipment or expanding the workforce significantly, and deal with downturns in demand without laying off workers.

Visits to Ford

Eiji Toyoda (born 1913), later president and then chairman at Toyota, and other Toyota executives visited the United States just after the resolution of the 1950 labor dispute. They toured Ford's River Rouge Plant, just outside Detroit, and other manufacturing sites. Their findings prompted them to undertake a five-year modernization program for plant and equipment.

Toyota's modernization program spanned the years from 1951 to 1955. It provided for doubling Toyota's production capacity, to 3,000 vehicles a month, largely by replacing antiquated equipment, installing conveyor lines, and automating processes. The additions included a continuous-casting line for engine blocks, large stamping machines, and multi-spot welding machines. Even the expanded capacity, however, remained minuscule in comparison with Ford's. A typical Ford assembly line at the time, operating with two shifts per day, turned out around 20,000 vehicles monthly.

The visitors from Toyota absorbed two important lessons at Ford. One was the value of soliciting employee suggestions for improvements in products and processes. Toyota implemented its own suggestion system in 1951. The other important lesson learned at Ford was the value of providing systematic training to production supervisors. All managers at Toyota, including workplace supervisors, began receiving education in Taylor-like scientific management in 1951. And by 1955, Toyota had included "takes the initiative in leading kaizen improvements" in the job description for workplace supervisors.

Quality control became part of the training curriculum for workplace supervisors at Toyota in 1953, and the company adopted a total quality control (TQC) program around 1960. Toyota had received complaints from the U.S. military that the quality of the vehicles it supplied was unsatisfactory. It had also received complaints from the Japanese government that quality levels at its suppliers were unacceptably low.

Toyota and other Japanese automakers began managing their purchasing systematically in the latter 1950s. They concentrated initially on evaluating suppliers' capacity for supplying sufficient quantities of parts on time and for achieving low defect rates and on providing guidance in tackling the necessary improvements. Only later did they address the issue of cost in managing their supplier relationships. Even the emphasis on quality failed, however, to prevent continuing problems with defective parts at Toyota as production volumes burgeoned.

Japan's first vehicle plant built expressly to produce passenger cars was Toyota's Motomachi Plant. That plant, opened near Toyota headquarters in 1959, was a fully integrated production platform, complete with stamping lines, body welding, paint shop, and vehicle assembly line. Motomachi had an initial production capacity of 5,000 cars a month and a target for increasing that capacity 10-fold within five years. It signified the Japanese automobile industry's coming of age in regard to matching the production capacity of U.S. vehicle plants.

Building the Motomachi Plant was something of a gamble in light of Toyota's sales volume at the time. But building it two or three years before any Japanese competitors built passenger car plants of comparable size proved prescient. The plant would be invaluable in enabling Toyota to increase its market share in Japan.

4. Shifting to Large-Scale Production

Family cars became common in Japan in the late 1960s. Vehicle sales in Japan, only about 400,000 in 1960, reached about 4 million in 1970. Japanese had entered the era of ubiquitous motor transport.

Accompanying the rapid growth in passenger car sales was equally rapid growth in the variety of models on offer. The increasing number of models meant that the production volume per model grew little, if at all, but the automakers managed to achieve viable costs through flexible manufacturing and productivity gains. They asserted those strengths in adopting short model cycles. In the 1960s, four years became the standard cycle for completely revamping principal models at Japan's larger automakers.

A shift in purchasing policy

Toyota and other automakers moved in the 1960s to support their surging production volumes by fostering economies of scale and other efficiencies in their purchasing. They allocated their purchasing contracts increasingly to specialized manufacturers. And rather than purchasing basic parts from numerous suppliers and assembling the parts themselves, they opted to purchase preassembled units from a limited number of suppliers. In addition, the automakers encouraged their suppliers to develop business with multiple automakers. That moderated the tendency toward automaker-specific groupings of suppliers and fostered a multilateral interchange among automakers and suppliers. It resulted in a complex web of relationships that has remained basically unchanged.

The successful primary suppliers became large, highly competitive corporations by specializing in selected categories of products and by developing business with multiple customers. Their suppliers—the secondary suppliers—remained smaller and handled mainly labor-intensive work. They typically employed fewer than 100 people and concentrated on the production of small-volume items or simple components or on individual steps in material processing. They handled work, in other words, that did not suit the primary suppliers' emphasis on economies of scale and high-value-added production. Their suppliers—the tertiary suppliers—and those suppliers' suppliers remained tiny enterprises, few of which employed more than 10 people. They handled the work that offered the lowest value-added.

In the 1960s, the automakers began managing costs systematically in purchasing parts. They encouraged suppliers to pursue continuing cost reductions through productivity gains and other kinds of improvements. Sources at Toyota report that the prices of parts purchased by the automaker declined, on average, about 30% between 1960 and 1965. Quality also remained an obsessive emphasis. Toyota extended its total quality control program to its suppliers in the latter 1960s. The quality of parts delivered to the automaker improved dramatically. That enabled Toyota to abandon the American-style approach of managing quality by inspecting all the parts that arrived from its suppliers. Instead, the principal suppliers took responsibility for ensuring the quality of their parts shipments and thereby relieved Toyota of the burden of conducting acceptance inspections.

5. Asserting International Competitiveness and Expanding Exports

The United States was the chief market for the stunning growth in Japan's vehicle exports in the 1970s. That growth initially caused little in the way of trade friction. The Japanese vehicles complemented, rather than displaced, the product offerings from the U.S. automakers. Small, fuel efficient, and affordable, they appealed to a large segment of the baby boomer generation—consumers who were eager to demonstrate a less-materialistic stance than that of their parents.

Detroit's automakers, meanwhile, were happy to continue serving the unashamedly materialistic demand for large cars. Those vehicles offered large profit margins, and the Big Three were content to leave the less-profitable small-car segment to the Japanese and other foreigners. Detroit remained complacent until big-car sales stalled after the second oil crisis, which occurred in 1979, and trade frictions would afflict U.S.-Japanese relations throughout the 1980s. Those frictions were to continue until the Japanese automakers and their suppliers had built massive supply capacity in North America.

In the meantime, automobiles became the subject of social scrutiny in the industrialized nations. Product safety became a serious issue, and automakers competed aggressively to demonstrate a commitment to preventing dangerous defects. Equally serious was the issue of pollution. Deteriorating air quality in Tokyo and other large Japanese cities occasioned tough new regulations on automotive exhaust emissions, and the oil crises focused unprecedented attention on the need for energy conservation.

The Japanese automakers temporarily slowed the pace of new-model launches and concentrated their resources on developing cleaner, more fuel efficient engine technologies. Among the technologies that emerged from that effort was Honda's compound vortex controlled combustion (CVCC). That breakthrough allowed Honda to meet U.S. emission standards in the 1970s without relying on catalytic converters. Another breakthrough technology was Toyota's three-way catalytic converter. That technology supplemented catalytic converters' traditional capacity for preventing emissions of carbon monoxide and hydrocarbons with the additional capacity for preventing emissions of nitrogen oxides.

Advances in engine technology provided a powerful and lasting competitive advantage for the Japanese automakers. Another advantage they honed in the 1970s was their capacity for securing viable profitability in the absence of industry expansion. Concerns arose after the first oil crisis, in 1973, that global growth in vehicle sales would cease. Those concerns prompted the Japanese automakers to undertake a new wave of cost cutting and automation. The concerns later proved unwarranted. But they engendered renewed advances in cost competitiveness and in flexibility. And those advances positioned the Japanese automakers to cope more effectively than their U.S. and European counterparts with subsequent fluctuations in demand.

Parts suppliers were active partners in the advances that the Japanese automakers achieved in cost competitiveness and in flexibility. The Japanese automakers relied on independent and semi-independent suppliers for between 70% and 80% of the parts and materials in their vehicles. Large and continuing reductions in costs became an absolute condition for the suppliers in maintaining business relationships with the automakers. The successful suppliers reinforced those relationships by synchronizing their operations with the pace of production at the vehicle plants. Toyota suppliers, for example, began using kanban information cards widely in the 1970s to manage production on a just-in-time basis. And Japanese automakers adopted online ordering with a growing number of suppliers during the decade.

6. Globalization

An unmistakable competitive advantage

The secret was out by the beginning of the 1980s. Japan's automakers had built a competitive edge over their U.S. and European rivals. They achieved an advantage first in productivity. But an equally compelling advantage in quality soon followed. Japanese models all but monopolized the top end of findings in third-party surveys of vehicle quality in the early 1980s.

We find that the Japanese automakers' cost advantage over the U.S. automakers in the U.S. market was greatest in 1985. It peaked just before the Plaza Accord, reached in September, produced a spike in the value of the yen against the dollar. Compact cars from Japan appear to have been $1,500 to $2,000 less expensive to make, ship, and sell in the United States than comparable U.S. models. The Big Three's offerings, in other words, were 30% to 40% more costly than competing Japanese models that cost $5,000 to make and deliver. That differential is attributable to the Japanese edge in productivity and—before the Plaza Accord—lower labor costs in Japan.

Small-car wars

Competition in the North American market turned nasty in the 1980s. The generally harmonious cohabitation between the U.S., European, and Japanese automakers that had prevailed until the 1970s became a battle for survival. Demand for big gas-guzzlers—Detroit's bread and butter—collapsed after the second oil crisis. The entire industry converged on European-style cars of compact size and monocoque bodies. All of the automakers were now competing for the same customers and in the same product categories. That concentrated competition became a permanent feature of the world automobile industry.

Recall, meanwhile, that a notable event in the 1980s was something that didn't happen. The widely predicted reinvention of the automobile never occurred. Progress in automotive technology accelerated as automakers adopted electronic control and new materials. But cars remained, as noted elsewhere, hunks of steel powered for the most part by gasoline engines. Progress was incremental rather than revolutionary. The Japanese automakers sharpened their competitive edge by accumulating and asserting strengths in bringing multifarious parts together in well-integrated products. European sophistication in vehicle design and performance had inspired a lot of the product development work in Japan. The Japanese had learned their lessons well and were now displaying unmatched attainment in product integrity.

In retrospect, the severe trade frictions that arose between the United States and Japan reflected a gap in capability building. The U.S. automakers finally recognized that the Japanese lead in capability building had spawned a huge differential in deep competitiveness, and they recognized that they needed time to catch up. We will take a close look at this subject in chapters 6 and 7.

International production and alliances

The Japanese automakers abandoned their nearly undeviating focus on vehicle exports and adopted a diversity of supply strategies in the 1980s.

They built vehicle plants in North America and in other markets outside Japan. They shared technology with overseas partners. Some produced vehicles with foreign partners in joint venture projects. Some produced and supplied vehicles for U.S. automakers to sell under their brands.

Nissan, Honda, and Toyota built wholly owned vehicle plants in North America, and Nissan built a vehicle plant in the United Kingdom. Toyota and General Motors in the United States and Nissan and Alfa Romeo in Italy produced cars together in joint ventures. Honda shared technology with British Leyland. Extensive sharing of parts and vehicles took place in relationships between Mitsubishi Motors and Chrysler, Isuzu and General Motors, Suzuki and General Motors, Mazda and Ford, Daihatsu and Innocenti, and Toyota and Lotus.

Vehicle production by the Japanese automakers outside Japan reached about 3 million vehicles in 1990 and would reach about 7 million in 2000. That growth in overseas production centered on North America. Just as striking as the growing number of Japanese vehicle plants on the North American landscape was the plethora of plants—more than 200 by 1990—being put up by Japanese manufacturers of automotive parts. Rarely in history had industry in any nation invested so heavily in another nation in such a short time span.

The machine that changed the world

Convincing documentation of the Japanese automakers' dominance in productivity and in other aspects of competitiveness appeared in the 1990 report of the Massachusetts Institute of Technology's International Motor Vehicle Program. That report captured attention worldwide as the best-selling book *The Machine That Changed the World*, penned mainly by James Womack and Daniel Jones. The book contained some exaggeration and a bit of oversimplification, but it was an epochal account of the strengths that the Japanese automakers had built in manufacturing, purchasing, product development, and other phases of the automobile business. It provided the first comprehensive explication of Toyota-style integrated production, and it popularized the term lean production as a description of Toyota's approach.

Public awareness of historical developments commonly lags behind the reality of those developments, and an awareness lag was much in evidence as the 1990s dawned. Still mired in recession on the eve of the information technology boom, many Americans saw "Japanese-style production" as the future. Worse, all too many Japanese believed their own PR and decided that the millennium was at hand and that they had nothing more to learn from the West. Largely unnoticed was the sharp slowdown that had occurred in productivity growth at the Japanese automakers, described in chapter 2. Also little noticed were the gains that the U.S. and European vehicle manufacturers were making in catching up with the Japanese.

The attention heaped on Japanese manufacturers proved valuable, nonetheless, in prompting objective analysis of the sources of their competitiveness. We will end our historical digression here and return in the next chapter to our examination of that competitiveness from the perspective of capability building.

5 Capability Building as an Emergent Process

The previous chapter was unashamedly anecdotal in examining how the Japanese automakers asserted a competitive edge in capability building. Here, we will adopt a more-rigorously analytical approach.

U.S. and European automakers began awakening in the early 1980s to the organizational capability that underlay the Japanese automakers' competitiveness. Industry executives, especially in the United States, had persisted stubbornly in attributing Japanese competitiveness entirely to lower wages. But by the end of the 1980s, nearly all of them were coming to terms with the real reason for the competitiveness gap. They were beginning to understand that gap as the result of differences in overall manufacturing systems. That newfound understanding preceded the gains that U.S. and European automakers began making toward narrowing the gap in the mid-1990s.

An unprecedented boom in vehicle demand inflated earnings in the U.S. automobile industry in the late 1990s, and the Big Three made the most of that boom through a successful strategy of concentrating on sales of pickup trucks and sport-utility vehicles. Some European automakers also achieved renewed vitality around the same time. They succeeded in coupling mass-production and mass marketing efficiencies with the kind of strong brand value formerly confined to small-volume prestige vehicles. Easy profits, however, were a curse in disguise. They diminished the sense of urgency about overcoming the Japanese edge in deep competitiveness, and the Japanese retained a competitive edge overall after the turn of the century.

1. The Concept of Emergence

Capability building as an emergent phenomenon

The Japanese automakers' production systems "emerged as the unplanned and unexpected result of ... seemingly unrelated innovations, improvements, and initiatives." That assertion in the previous chapter is essential to understanding those systems and the organizational capability that underlies the systems.

That chapter's further assertions that "the Japanese had no idea ... what they were doing" and that "the systems emerged through piecemeal, ad hoc measures for addressing needs and issues" are at odds with conventional economic theory. Economists and management theorists have tended to describe organizational capability as the result of conscious decisions. A popular interpretation has characterized those decisions as choices made in the name of achieving goals amid constraints.

Rational decision making by self-optimizing economic units might be a useful place to begin in analyzing the Japanese automakers' production systems. But that hypothesis soon proves inadequate to explain the reality that we encounter in the workplace at the Japanese automakers. It certainly conflicts with the accounts offered by veterans of Japanese automobile manufacturing.

The operative principle in the author's interpretation of organizational capability building at the Japanese automakers is "emergence." Scientists invoke that principle, as we saw in chapter 1, in reference to complex phenomena that arise unpredictably from simpler rules. The principle performs admirably well in accounting for the evolution of the Japanese automakers' production systems. That those systems are internationally competitive is beyond dispute. But their competitiveness clearly emerged—notwithstanding the bold dreams of visionaries like Kiichiro Toyoda—as after-the-fact economic rationality rather than as the planned result of advance decision making.

The diverse paths of emergence

Japan's automakers, like all manufacturers, have employed diverse approaches to capability building in production and in product development. Some of those approaches, to be sure, have evinced the rational calculation of systematic planning. Managements, that is, have sometimes analyzed the constraints imposed by the competitive environment and reshaped their capabilities systematically with an eye to addressing those constraints. But their approaches have more often addressed competitive challenges less systematically and occasionally even randomly (fig. 5-1).

FIGURE 5-1

Paths of Emergence in the Development of the Toyota Production System

Rational calculation

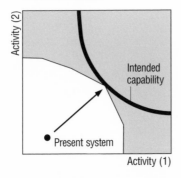

Random trials

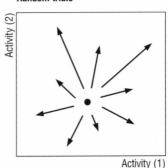

Induction by environmental constraints

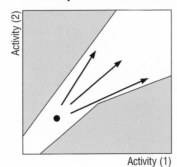

Entrepreneurial vision

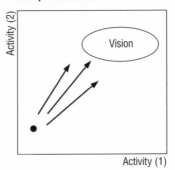

Knowledge transfer

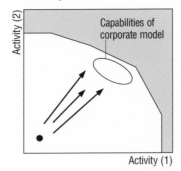

FIGURE 5-2

Representative Elements of the Toyota Production System and their Paths of Emergence

Path \ Element	Just-in-time production	Multiskill training, multitask personnel deployment, equipment deployment by product	Deployment of automated and flexible equipment	Continual kaizen improvements and total quality control (TQC)	Parts purchasing based on drawings generated by parts manufacturers and approved by automakers	Powerful product managers (shusa, "chief engineers")
Entrepreneurial vision and innovation	Conceived by Kiichiro Toyoda in 1930s and put into practice by Taiichi Ohno in 1940s and 1950s	Kiichiro Toyoda's 1945 call for raising productivity 10-fold in three years	Kiichiro Toyoda's call in 1930s for achieving costs in Japanese small-volume production comparable to those in U.S. large-volume production	Top-down introduction of TQC, spearheaded by Eiji Toyoda and others; little Toyota originality initially	Kiichiro Toyoda's 1930s call for promoting development of specialized parts manufacturers, an initiative of admittedly uncertain results	
Knowledge transfer from other industries		Textile industry's multitasking practice of assigning single operator to multiple machines	Automated features developed by Sakichi Toyoda for looms	TQC benefits as demonstrated in other manufacturing industries and as promoted by Union of Japanese Scientists and Engineers and by others	Practices characteristic of prewar dealings between assembly manufacturers and parts manufacturers in train of aircraft industries	Borrowing of chief designer system from aircraft industry; postwar influx of aircraft engineers
Knowledge transfer from Ford system and from scientific management	Synchronization of work in multiple processes (predating installation of conveyor lines)	Productivity benchmarking against Ford; adoption of standardized work as form of modified Taylorism	Introduction of Detroit-style transfer machines on mass production lines for engines and other core components	Ford's employee suggestion system; human resources development through in-house training; introduction of statistical quality control		
The need to expand production volume while coping with input limitations	1940s: resumption of production with surviving equipment 1950s: serious labor dispute and subsequent restraint in hiring in connection with pledge to guarantee employment 1960s: rapid growth in production volume 1970s: development of management methods for maintaining efficiency and profitability through fluctuations in production volume		Development of low-cost automation to cope with limited availability of investment funding	Intensive in-house training in 1950s to address shortage of workplace supervisors for replacing increasingly outmoded craftsperson-like leadership	Pressure to outsource design work accompanying explosive diversification in vehicle models in 1960s	
Small and fragmented local market	Development of measures for calling attention to accumulating product inventories; introduction of kanban as emulation of conveyor-based synchronization	Need for cultivating multiskilled workers in support of producing multiple models in small volumes	Automated responses to need for producing multiplicity of products in small volumes		Outsourcing of design responsibilities for electrical parts as result of Toyota's spin-off of Nippondenso (now Denso) in 1949	
Insufficient capacity for absorbing skills and technology	Lack of access to world-class computerization for supporting production control		Low level of computerized control in early stages of extensive automation; simple measures for detecting problems and stopping equipment when problems occurred			
Competitive pressure	Measures for highlighting problems and promoting kaizen improvements; measures for shortening lead time, raising productivity, improving quality, and reducing inventories	Need for raising productivity without relying on heavy investment in new equipment or in new technology	Measures for highlighting problems and promoting kaizen improvements; focus on cost efficiency and flexibility	Continual progress in improving quality and raising productivity; measures for motivating employees and for invigorating organization	Adoption of parts designs that favored easier, less-expensive manufacturing; advances in shortening lead time and raising productivity in product development	High level of product integrity; short lead time and high productivity in product development
Benefits recognized after the fact		Including several advances conceived originally at Toyota, such as measures for calling attention to problems, flexibility in deploying personnel engendered by multiskill training and multitasking, and U-shaped layouts		Conscious building of framework at Toyota—not exceptionally early in adopting TQC—for maintaining TQC activities even after earning Deming Prize for quality management	Innovation at Toyota—not especially early in outsourcing parts design work to suppliers—in refining outsourcing framework and in delineating responsibility for quality assurance	Earlier (1950s) and more sweeping adoption of product manager format at Toyota than at other automakers, though all automakers hired former aircraft engineers and most employed product manager format

Induction by environmental constraints

Capability building has frequently consisted of little more than trial and error—an approach that has a proud and fertile tradition in the Japanese automobile industry. It has sometimes been a matter of coping with severe restraints, as when Japan's automakers went to work with antiquated and limited equipment after World War II. The automakers have occasionally built capabilities in accordance with the entrepreneurial zeal of their leaders, but any strategic genius subsequently attributed to their accomplishments has ordinarily become evident only after the fact. Another source of progress in capability building has been know-how acquired from competitors through licensing, imitation, or other means. The likely contributions of acquired know-how to capability building have rarely been known or even knowable at the time of the acquisition.

Executives and employees, struggling with the daily exigencies of business, have little time to think about which approach they are using. At best, they press ahead doggedly, choosing what appears to be the better course at each fork in the road. Any alleged logic in their progress is little more than a description of what happened, usually in retrospect. Blind perseverance is as good a description as any for the postwar progress of Japan's best automakers in capability building.

2. The Birth of Characteristically Japanese Production Systems

Figure 5-2 summarizes our after-the-fact findings about diverse paths by which important elements of the Toyota Production System emerged. Note the vast range of stimuli that occasions advances in the system. The table identifies crucial advances that resulted from entrepreneurial vision; from borrowings from other industries; from borrowings from other automakers; from rational calculation; from the systemization of advances recognized after the fact; and—most notably—from the severe restraints imposed by Japan's fledgling automobile market.

We have seen that constraints imposed by the underdeveloped Japanese market inspired innovative approaches in maximizing economies of scale, in seeking flexibility in manufacturing, and in avoiding excessive capital spending. And we have seen how those approaches ultimately helped make Toyota and the other Japanese automakers internationally competitive. Following is a summary of some of the principal constraints imposed on the Japanese automakers by their domestic market. We should resist the temptation to romanticize the automakers' response to adversity. We need to bear in mind that no one at the automakers regarded any of the restraints as a blessing in disguise. People who were present at the time recall thinking that they could do better if only the market were bigger and capital more readily available.

Labor input

The Japanese automakers increased their unit output greatly from the 1950s to the 1980s while contending with chronic shortages of labor. This is not to suggest that Japan suffered from a labor shortage throughout the period in question. Rather, when labor was plentiful the automakers lacked the fiscal latitude to hire freely, and the labor-management covenant that emerged in the 1950s prevented them from hiring casually and laying people off when demand declined. By the time the automakers had gained the wherewithal to hire more freely, the booming Japanese economy had made labor hard to come by.

Gains in labor productivity, as we have seen, are basically of two kinds: raising efficiency in transferring information to material and increasing the percentage of working hours employed in transferring information. Toyota and the other Japanese automakers were notably successful in the latter kind of productivity gains; that is, in minimizing the amount of paid time not employed directly in producing salable products.

Versatility

Adam Smith famously preached the value of specialization in raising productivity, and American-style mass production—based on specialization and narrowly defined job descriptions—dominated world markets in the first half of the 20th century. Excessive specialization, however, was a reason for the subsequent decline in the international competitiveness of U.S. manufacturing. Deploying labor and equipment narrowly and rigidly reduces overall productivity. It creates inefficiencies in factories by preventing processes from interacting smoothly.

Shortages of labor and equipment in the 1950s obliged Japan's automakers to assign each worker and to deploy each machine to handle a broad range of work. Circumstances thus prevented the automakers from using as much specialization as they surely would have preferred and surely would have used had they been able. Avoiding overspecialization was an emphasis in the reengineering espoused by several American management theorists in the 1990s. Japanese automakers had long ago learned that lesson well. They had learned it through practice and without the benefit of theoretical conceptualizing. Note that worker versatility was instrumental in maximizing the amount of paid time directly employed in generating value.

Suppliers

In purchasing, chronic shortages of labor prompted the Japanese automakers to (1) outsource a large portion of their parts production and (2) rely on specialized suppliers. Some people at the automakers bristled at the thought of loosening their hands-on control over the production of important parts, but the surging production volumes and multiplying vehicle models of the 1960s overruled their objections: the automakers simply didn't have enough resources to continue making or even designing as many of their parts as they had previously. And since the purpose of the outsourcing was to streamline operations for the automakers, the purchase orders went increasingly to suppliers who possessed sophisticated, specialized capabilities in designing and producing complete functional units.

The automakers' preference would have been to continue making more, rather than fewer, parts at their own plants. Circumstances forced them, however, to act contrary to their instincts. Here again, the result was an unexpected increase in competitiveness: the suppliers achieved continuing improvements in productivity and in design sophistication, and the automakers ended up obtaining better parts at lower prices than they could have produced on their own.

Capital spending

We have seen that Japan's cash-starved automakers needed to make do with old equipment as they resumed production after World War II. Unable to invest heavily in plant and equipment, they needed to rely on inexpensive improvements, mainly in methods, to ramp up production. Everyone in the plants became responsible for inspecting and maintaining the equipment that they used. Everyone took part in identifying ways to improve the way things worked. They modified production processes and product designs and did everything else humanly possible to optimize the flow of production.

The Japanese automakers' early focus on increasing output with a minimum of investment established a lasting pattern of thrift in capital spending. That thrift would serve them well in subsequent global competition. It was yet another competitive strength that arose from onerous and unavoidable constraints.

Model lines

The experiences of the U.S. and Japanese automobile industries in their formative years are a study in contrasts, and the most-conspicuous contrast is in model line strategies. Annual production of Ford's Model T, introduced in 1908, reached nearly 2 million units in 1923 and 1924. Japan's automakers came of age as international competitors in the late 1970s and in the 1980s. During those years, Toyota's production of its core models averaged only around 200,000 vehicles a year. That is the volume generally regarded as the minimum for operating automotive production systems optimally in Japan. Annual production in the Japanese automobile industry overall averaged only about 130,000 vehicles per passenger car model in the mid-1980s.

As we have seen, growth in the number of Japanese passenger car models offset overall unit growth and curtailed growth in production volume per model. Japanese passenger car models and model variations multiplied as domestic demand burgeoned in the 1960s, and further diversification in model specifications occurred as Japan's automakers expanded the volume and the geographical scope of their exports in the 1970s. A new round of model diversification took place in the 1980s, driven by Japan's bubble economy.

Model categories in Japan are clear-cut, and consumers have a firm notion of which models from which automakers occupy each category. The result is intense, head-to-head competition across the entire model spectrum. That pattern of aggressive, model-by-model competition has raised the stakes in deploying model lines efficiently. It has honed the competitive edge developed—out of necessity—in asserting flexible efficiency in support of diverse product offerings. And that competitive edge in flexibility has been a definitive advantage for the Japanese automakers in the global marketplace.

Product development

Deploying comprehensive model lines and revamping the main models every four years—the shortest model cycle in the world automobile industry—left Japan's automakers with a chronic shortage of engineers in their design and development divisions. The unwelcome constraints of insufficient manpower and unyielding development deadlines obliged the automakers to find ways to raise efficiency.

The short development schedules, for example, meant designing the production processes for upcoming models while the models were still in development. That concurrent engineering fostered and reinforced close communication between the product development people and their counterparts in production engineering and in purchasing. The Japanese automakers would benefit hugely from that good communication among functions.

Entrepreneurial vision

Visionary leadership can steer companies toward great accomplishments despite an astonishing disregard for the practical constraints faced by the companies. That happened at Toyota under Kiichiro Toyoda and at Honda under founder Soichiro Honda (1906–1991). Both of those companies built organizational capability that proved an eminently rational response to competitive pressures. Neither leader accompanied their exciting vision, however, with a particularly convincing or reassuring program for fulfilling the vision.

Toyoda issued his dramatic call for attaining U.S.-level productivity at Japanese-level production volumes before his company possessed a vehicle plant. None of his tactics—even those that we recognize in retrospect as progenitors of just-in-time production—offered the faintest promise of overtaking Ford or General Motors. Yet Toyoda's dream of raising productivity without relying on economies of scale clearly defined his company's subsequent development. Toyota's productivity rose impressively during the first 10 years after World War II in the absence of comparable growth in production scale. And after large-scale demand finally arrived in Japan in the 1960s, Toyota's productivity delivered genuinely world-class efficiency.

Borrowed know-how: from Ford

Toyota's production system differed strikingly from Ford's in (1) using just-in-time production to minimize inventories of parts and (2) empowering people in the workplace to take the initiative in improving processes. Those and other differences have caused all too many observes to conclude wrongly that the Toyota Production System arose as a rejection of Fordism. In fact, the Toyota system is more an extension than a rejection of the Ford system.

Ford's production system was long a model for Toyota and Japan's other automakers. Protectionist industrial policies shielded Japan's automakers from foreign competition from 1936 to the 1960s. In the absence of direct foreign competition, Toyota and the other Japanese automakers monitored their competitiveness against virtual competitors. Their attention centered on Ford, and they benchmarked their products and productivity carefully against Ford's. When Kiichiro Toyoda and Taiichi Ohno discussed their productivity relative to American levels, they had Ford in mind.

The obsession with Ford is understandable. Toyoda, Ohno, and others in the Japanese automobile industry cut their teeth at a time when Ford and General Motors dominated the Japanese market. After the war, they borrowed heavily from Ford in adopting the U.S. automaker's conveyor line assembly, its transfer machines for moving parts from one automated process to the next, and even its suggestion system. The preoccupation with Ford surely figured in broader borrowings from the United States, including Taylor's standardized work, training in scientific management for workplace supervisors, and statistical quality control.

We should presumably regard most of the borrowings from Ford and from other U.S. sources as examples of rational calculation and planned capability building. The Japanese automakers knew, for the most part, what they were getting and why. Rational calculation is evident in the way they modified the U.S. practices from the start to accommodate Japanese circumstances, including financial and technological limitations.

Borrowed know-how: from textile manufacturing

Rational calculation is also apparent in a fateful recruitment from the textile industry: Taiichi Ohno. The father of the Toyota Production System worked at Toyoda Boshoku, a spinning company, before moving to Toyota Motor. At his former employer, Ohno and colleagues bench-marked their productivity against that of a stronger competitor, Dainippon Spinners (now Unitika). They discovered that their competitor produced yarn in smaller lots than they were using, that it equipped its production systems with built-in features for preventing defects, and that it deployed its production equipment by product rather than by process. Toyoda Boshoku promptly adopted those practices to good effect.

Ohno found the production control at Toyota Motor less advanced than what he was accustomed to in the spinning industry. His experience at Toyoda Boshoku lay behind the now-legendary improvements he made in his machining shop at the automobile company. Those improvements—such assigning individual workers to multiple tasks and rearranging equipment by product—mirrored similar, earlier measures at the spinning company.

Borrowed know-how: from aircraft manufacturing

A windfall for Japan's fledgling automobile industry was the postwar influx of engineering talent from the aeronautics sector. Aircraft manufacturing had absorbed the cream of Japanese engineering talent during the war years, and technological standards for products and for manufacturing were far higher in that sector than in vehicle manufacturing. The occupation authorities forced Japan to dismantle its aircraft industry, however, and a lot of the displaced engineers sought employment in the automotive sector.

Toyota's inheritance from the aircraft industry included the practice of conducting product development projects under all-powerful product managers. Those managers, known as chief engineers at Toyota, wielded immense cross-functional authority. They proved immensely influential in Toyota's development. Incidentally, the chief engineer for the first-generation Corolla was a former aircraft engineer.

A powerful product manager—"chief designer" in the parlance of Japan's wartime aircraft makers—is especially important in aircraft engineering. Achieving a finely tuned balance among diverse aeronautic systems is of supreme importance in optimizing aircraft performance. That kind of balance became indispensable in automotive engineering in the 1980s. Automakers faced daunting requirements in regard to safety, emissions, and fuel economy, and optimizing the interaction of vehicle systems was essential to fulfilling those requirements.

The sweeping authority vested in the chief engineer contributed visibly to Toyota's increasingly manifest edge in development productivity, in development lead time, and in overall product competitiveness. Powerful product managers also arose at other Japanese automakers, and they sometimes asserted authority as broad as that wielded by their Toyota counterparts. But only Toyota instituted the omnipotent product manager as a standard fixture in product development.

Interestingly, the chief engineer system offered little advantage over other ways of managing product development when Toyota adopted the system. Japan's other automakers did more or less as well as Toyota in product development from the 1950s to the 1970s. Only when technological demands escalated sharply in the 1980s did the competitive advantage of Toyota's chief engineer system become evident and widely imitated. This is yet another example of the uncanny emergence of organizational capability and of competitiveness based on that capability.

3. A Culture of Alertness and Preparedness

Most companies strive to grow and prosper. All of them encounter challenges and opportunities, and all of them acquire capabilities for addressing those challenges and opportunities. All of them acquire their capabilities through a combination of foresight, effort, and luck. The foregoing discussion of planned and unplanned, intended and unintended advances in capability building begs the question: Why, with so much happenstance at work, should one company (Toyota) or group of companies (the Japanese automakers) consistently outperform its or their rivals in capability building and, by extension, in competitiveness?

Something that distinguishes Toyota from other automakers is its culture of alertness and preparedness. Management at Toyota has no crystal ball secreted away in the boardroom, and the people in the Toyota workplace enjoy no special clairvoyance in tackling improvements. What we discover everywhere at Toyota, however, is a continual questioning: How can this make us better?; a willingness to try anything; a readiness to adopt whatever seems to work; and a practice of propagating good ideas throughout the company. An improvement that works well anywhere in Toyota's operations soon turns up at workplaces throughout the organization.

Toyota's great strength resides not in just-in-time production or any other method or device but in the company's capacity for creating and applying effective tools, useful capabilities. Toyota would remain a powerful competitor even if it abandoned all of its famous methods. Its unexcelled capacity for building capabilities would soon spawn new and equally potent methods. Elucidating that capacity is a fiendishly difficult undertaking, but it is the only way to come to terms with the real source of Toyota's competitiveness.

6 Competition, Conflict, and Cooperation

This book is ultimately about competition: the capability-building competition that ensues when managements recognize capability building as the wellspring of surface competitiveness. Competition is inherently brutal, and it inevitably entails conflict.

Automobile industry-related news articles from the 1980s and 1990s are replete with references to escalating global competition; festering trade disputes; and—incongruously—multiplying and deepening cross-border partnerships between automakers. We have grown accustomed to the notion of accompanying competition with collaboration and have become inured to the incongruity of their simultaneity. Yet we have learned, at least since the time of Adam Smith, to be wary of cooperation among supposed competitors. We expect companies to serve our interests as consumers by concentrating on competition, and we expect the authorities to help by enforcing laws for preventing collusion. The simultaneous competition, conflict, and cooperation that occurred in the 1980s and 1990s and the influence of that combination on capability building warrant careful consideration.

1. Trade Frictions

We examined several constraints in the preceding chapter that prompted responses by Toyota and by the other Japanese automakers, and we saw how those responses strengthened the automakers in planned and in unplanned ways. Trade frictions, too, were a constraint in the competitive environment for the Japanese automakers in the 1980s and 1990s. Like the other constraints, trade frictions prompted responses by the Japanese automakers. And yes, those responses also had the effect of making the Japanese automakers even more competitive. Heavy investment by the automakers and by their Japanese suppliers in North American and European manufacturing has largely eased the frictions, but the lessons of the trade disputes remain instructive in the context of capability building.

In no industry does history offer any instances of protectionist measures restoring the vitality of companies that had become uncompetitive. Import restrictions prompted by trade frictions have exerted only auxiliary influence on the long-term development of the automobile industry. What has shaped the industry's development decisively has been internal capability building at the automakers, not external artifice by governments.

The so-called voluntary export restraint by Japan's automakers, beginning in the early 1980s, undeniably affected the automobile industry. That restraint presented the U.S. automakers with a reprieve in capability-building competition and let them secure artificially inflated profits at the expense of American consumers. But any long-term results of such measures hinge on efforts by the beneficiaries to achieve renewed progress in capability building.

We will focus on the U.S.-Japanese trade relationship in our examination of trade frictions in the automobile industry. The protectionist moves in that relationship were basically consistent with the emergency measures agreed among nations and institutionalized in the General Agreement on Tariffs and Trade and in its successor, the World Trade Organization. We will disregard unilateral measures taken outside those trade regimes. Those unilateral moves include the limits imposed by France on vehicle imports from Japan and the import-substitution policies adopted by developing nations to promote the development of domestic automobile industries.

Let us bear in mind, meanwhile, that "the Americans" and "the Japanese" were anything but seamless unities. The U.S. distributors of imported cars saw things in a very different light, for example, from the Big Three U.S. automakers and the United Auto Workers. Differences, at least in nuance, were also perceptible among the Japanese.

Tit for tat

Predictably, the U.S. automakers, U.S. labor leaders, and U.S. legislators blamed the widening trade imbalance in the automotive sector on unfair practices by the Japanese. Just as predictably, the Japanese blamed the trend on insufficient effort by the U.S. automakers. Here is some pertinent background (fig. 6-1).

FIGURE 6-1

U.S. and Japanese Interpretations of the Consequences of Different Factors in the Market Performance of the U.S. Automakers

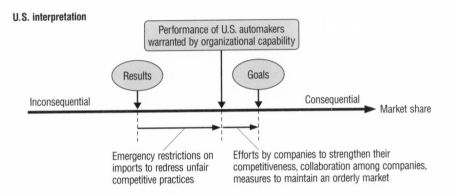

U.S. interpretation

Performance of U.S. automakers warranted by organizational capability

Results — Goals

Inconsequential — Consequential — Market share

Emergency restrictions on imports to redress unfair competitive practices

Efforts by companies to strengthen their competitiveness, collaboration among companies, measures to maintain an orderly market

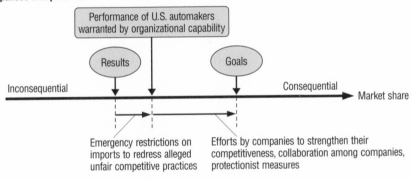

Japanese interpretation

Performance of U.S. automakers warranted by organizational capability

Results — Goals

Inconsequential — Consequential — Market share

Emergency restrictions on imports to redress alleged unfair competitive practices

Efforts by companies to strengthen their competitiveness, collaboration among companies, protectionist measures

Japan imposed higher import tariffs on vehicles than most other industrialized nations until 1969. It subsequently lowered those tariffs incrementally and had essentially eliminated its import tariffs on vehicles by 1978. By 1980, Japan had also eliminated its import tariffs on nearly all automotive components.

The American critics of Japan, denied an issue in tariffs, turned their attention to alleged nontariff trade barriers. They blamed those supposed obstacles for the failure of the U.S. automakers to make inroads in the Japanese market while the Japanese automakers were making hay in the

U.S. market. The U.S.-Japanese governmental agreement of 1980 called for Japan to streamline import procedures and otherwise ease market access for U.S. vehicles. Subsequent bilateral negotiations addressed the U.S. assertions of "structural impediments" in the Japanese market, such as exclusive sales channels.

Japanese automakers moved in the 1990s to arrange for their domestic dealers to handle U.S. vehicles; notably, General Motors cars at Toyota dealers, Fords at Mazda dealers, and Chryslers at Honda dealers. Japan's automakers also issued plans for increasing their purchasing from non-Japanese suppliers. In 1995, the U.S. government pressed Japan for increases in the amount of U.S. purchasing by the Japanese automakers and for increases in the number of Japanese dealers that would handle U.S. vehicles.

What emerged amid the escalating tit for tat of trade negotiations was the inevitability of large-scale U.S. production by the Japanese automakers. By the end of the 1980s, the Japanese automakers were producing vehicles at wholly owned North American plants in Ohio (Honda); Tennessee (Nissan); Kentucky and Ontario (Toyota), and Indiana (Isuzu and Fuji Heavy Industries [Subaru] jointly). They were producing vehicles at joint ventures with American partners in California (Toyota and General Motors); Michigan (Mazda and Ford); Illinois (Mitsubishi Motors and Chrysler); and Ontario (Suzuki and General Motors). And the aggregate production capacity of the Japanese-affiliated plants had reached 2 million vehicles a year.

Engaging in North American production enabled the Japanese automakers and their suppliers to localize their capability building. The joint ventures—which invariably relied on production technology provided by the Japanese partner—enabled the U.S. automakers, meanwhile, to undertake renewed capability building.

Shifting modes of negotiation

The focus of the U.S.-Japanese trade dispute in the automotive sector shifted in 1980 to comprehensive government negotiations, from individual complaints. Big-car sales in the United States had recovered by 1976, and that had temporarily dampened the rancor over Japanese imports. But emotions boiled over again after the second oil crisis, in

1979. The market share for imported vehicles in the United States surged past the 20% mark, led by fuel-efficient compact cars, and Japanese vehicles accounted for the majority of the imports. Japan and its automakers again became the subjects of vociferous attack.

A flurry of government and industry negotiations ensued. The upshot was a package of Japanese government concessions that defused the incipient crisis for the time being. That suited the U.S. government, which was still eager to demonstrate a commitment to free trade, a stance later abandoned. The United Auto Workers and Ford, dissatisfied with the governmental solution, filed complaints with the U.S. government's International Trade Commission, which the commission narrowly rejected.

Powerful senators then introduced legislation that would have imposed a ceiling on Japanese vehicle imports for three years. Armed with that legislative threat, the Reagan administration induced Japan's government to persuade its automakers to limit their U.S. exports. The "voluntary export restraint" by the Japanese automakers, begun in 1981, continued until 1994. That pattern of complaint filings, legislative threats, and government negotiations set the tone for U.S.-Japanese trade negotiations into the 1990s.

The export restraint by Japan's automakers raised costs artificially for American consumers, and independent studies have been nearly unanimous in concluding that the net effect on the U.S. economy was harmful. Political pressure yielded the important benefit, though, of prompting the Japanese automakers to build and expand production capacity in North America. Their North American manufacturing operations were generally successful and thus demonstrated the potential for replicating Japanese capability building outside Japan. They exposed the disingenuousness of attributing the competitiveness of Japanese imports to structural advantages supposedly resident in Japan. And they stimulated capability building at the Big Three automakers' North American plants. The responses induced by trade frictions resulted in a more-even international distribution of manufacturing capability in the automobile industry.

2. Cooperation

Automakers engage in cooperation to leverage their strengths through complementary specialization and to reinforce their competitiveness in areas—for example, sales and service in new and unfamiliar markets, emissions-control technologies, etc.—where they are weak. Cooperation can also be a means, as noted, of addressing the constraints of political pressure that arise from trade frictions. Effective relationship building is, in itself, an important aspect of an automaker's strategic competence.

The cast

Our interest here is in external cooperation among autonomous passenger car manufacturers—automakers who possess unique brands, possess stand-alone capabilities for developing and manufacturing engines and bodies, deploy lineups of independently developed models, and deploy dealer networks for marketing and servicing those models. The automakers that fulfill our definition include highly independent companies, such as General Motors, Toyota, and Volkswagen; companies in which other automakers hold large minority stakes, such as Fuji Heavy Industries (Subaru) and Mazda; and automakers that operate as majority-owned subsidiaries of other automakers, such as Chrysler, Daihatsu, and Volvo.

The number of automakers that qualify as autonomous under our definition has declined in recent decades, but it remains far larger than envisioned by numerous pundits. Prominent journalists, securities analysts, and even industry executives have long prophesized an industry shakeout that would narrow the field to no more than 10 automakers. A survey by the author and Akira Takeishi, of Hitotsubashi University, identified 20 autonomous automakers in 1999. That number was down from 27 in 1990 and 30 in 1980, but it was still double the high-end figure suggested by the shakeout prophets. The industry has thus proved persistently and, to some, surprisingly resilient in its diversity.

Mere economies of scale would appear to be less decisive than the conventional wisdom decreed. Studies and experience suggest that the smallest optimal volume for a mass-production passenger car model is about 200,000 vehicles annually. Automakers need multiple models, of course, to stabilize their sales and earnings performance, but annual production of 2 million vehicles would seem to afford ample economies of scale to ensure viability for an automaker. Global automobile production in the late 1990s was around 50 million vehicles a year, so the numerical basis for the shakeout prophecies is highly suspect.

Equally suspect is the notion that massive scale is necessary to support R&D work on increasingly sophisticated power train, safety, and other crucial technologies. Long-range development work on basic technologies consumes a small percentage of automakers' R&D budgets. And the automakers share the costs of the most expensive research, such as work on fuel cells, through international consortiums and other kinds of cooperation. Most of the automakers' R&D spending goes into short-range product development, which consists mainly of applying well-established technologies in new models.

The shakeout prophecies also reveal, in retrospect, a disregard for the role of capability building in asserting and maintaining competitiveness. Japan is home to nearly one-half of the world's autonomous manufacturers of passenger cars. Our definition leaves room for debate about the number of companies that qualify as autonomous, but the Japanese qualifiers number at least eight. That is a large number in view of the size of Japan's domestic market. It demonstrates convincingly the organizational capability built by the automakers in support of manufacturing numerous models in small volumes per model.

Supplementary capability building through cooperation is another reason for the survival of numerous automakers in Japan. The smaller automakers have enjoyed access, for example, to the larger automakers' parts purchasing systems. In addition, most of Japan's smaller automakers established alliances with larger automakers in the 1960s and 1970s, which have bolstered their viability. This same basic pattern is yet another reason for the resiliently large number of autonomous automakers worldwide. Each automaker has been able to buttress its survivability by supplementing its core competence through cooperation. Long-term survival still depends, however, on individual, internal, and independent progress in capability building.

Lots of ways to work together

The world's automakers engaged in more than 100 formal collaborations with each other—more than 5 per automaker—as of 2000 (fig. 6-2). Those ties included equity holdings of varying percentages; joint ventures; and other modes of cooperation in R&D, production, and marketing. As shown in figure 6-2, the number of collaborations increased greatly from

FIGURE 6-2

Collaborations among Automakers*

Year and location of active partner**		Location of passive partner**			Kind of collaboration**				Total
		Japan	United States	Europe	Equity investment	Joint venture	Joint R&D or joint production	Marketing collaboration	
1985	Japan	4	8	1	4	1	7	1	13
	U.S.A.	5	0	0	4	1	0	0	5
	Europe	1	3	14	1	8	8	1	18
	Total	10	11	15	9	10	5	2	36
1990	Japan	8	19	15	5	11	15	11	42
	U.S.A.	10	2	3	5	7	2	1	15
	Europe	8	2	35	2	6	37	0	45
	Total	26	23	53	12	24	54	12	102
1995	Japan	14	15	16	2	9	25	9	45
	U.S.A.	9	2	5	4	8	3	1	16
	Europe	8	4	39	1	15	35	0	51
	Total	31	21	60	7	32	63	10	112
1998	Japan	15	14	9	2	9	24	3	38
	U.S.A.	10	2	6	6	8	3	1	18
	Europe	6	4	39	3	13	33	0	49
	Total	31	20	54	11	30	60	4	105

* The automakers covered in the table number 20: Daihatsu, Fuji Heavy Industries (Subaru), Honda, Mazda, Mitsubishi Motors, Nissan, Suzuki, and Toyota in Japan; the former Chrysler, Ford, and General Motors in the United States; BMW, Fiat, the former Mercedes-Benz, PSA, Renault, Rover, Saab, Volkswagen, and Volvo in Europe. The numbers for 1998 reflect Ford's 1999 acquisition of Volvo's passenger car operations and Renault's purchase of a controlling interest in Nissan, also in 1999.

** "Passive partner" refers to the recipient of investment, technology, or other support through a collaboration; "active partner" refers to the source of the investment or support. In regard to joint ventures and other largely reciprocal collaborations, each partner appears in the numbers as an active partner and as a passive partner. The numbers include only a single listing for partners that have multiple collaborations with each other. Collaborations in regions other than Japan, the United States, or Europe do not appear in the numbers.

Source: T. Fujimoto and A. Takeishi (2003), based on Jidosha Sangyo Handobukku (Automobile Industry Handbook), annual editions, Nikkan Jidosha Shimbunsha

the mid-1980s to the early 1990s, and most of that increase occurred in loose arrangements of limited scope.

Cooperation fortified the automakers' capabilities in every phase of generating value (fig. 6-3). No automaker is the best at everything or the worst at everything. Every automaker has reinforced some aspect of its capability through cooperation, and all of the principal automakers have supplemented their competence at different levels of their organizations and in different functions through multiple collaborations.

The European automakers were the first to engage in cooperation widely. By the early 1980s, Renault, for instance, was developing automatic

FIGURE 6-3
Collaboration at Different Levels

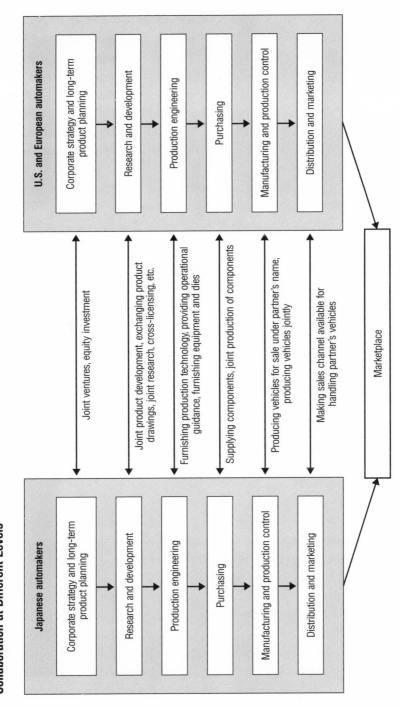

transmissions with Volkswagen, developing diesel engines with Fiat, cross-licensing parts with British Leyland, and conducting joint R&D and joint production with Volvo. Europe's other automakers engaged in similarly multilateral cooperation, and the entire European automobile industry was a veritable web of cooperative networking.

The Japanese automakers emerged as active and important participants in corporate collaboration in the 1980s. Their participation helped establish once and for all a truly global mesh of cooperative relationships in the automobile industry.

Outright mergers and acquisitions, including speculation about potential perpetrators and targets, received extensive and sensational media coverage. Belying the media frenzy was the small number of automakers that actually took the plunge. Most of the mergers and acquisitions in recent decades have been complementary affairs in which automakers sought to round out their product lines: Ford with Jaguar and with Volvo, General Motors with Saab, Daimler-Benz with Chrysler, Chrysler with American Motors, BMW with Rover (since annulled), Fiat with Lancia and Alfa Romeo, Volkswagen with Audi.

Mergers and acquisitions between manufacturers of similarly positioned mass-market vehicles have been rare. The chief examples have been Volkswagen with Seat and with Skoda, Peugeot with Citroën, Hyundai with Kia, and Nissan with Prince. To whatever extent those mergers have succeeded, they have succeeded more through combining complementary model lines than through amplifying economies of scale.

Regional trends

American capital was conspicuous in the high-profile capital investments among automakers in the 1970s and 1980s. Most of the acquisitions of niche manufacturers by mass-market producers were European investments by U.S. automakers; notably, Ford in Jaguar and in Volvo and General Motors in Saab. The U.S. automakers were using their still-potent capital clout to obtain the strong brands of financially weak European counterparts.

Japan's automakers figured initially in the cross-border movements of capital as investees, rather than as investors. Minority equity stakes, rather than outright acquisitions, characterized the investments, and the partners were usually U.S. automakers. Those moves followed Japan's loosening of restrictions on inward investment in the early 1970s. They included minority investments by General Motors in Isuzu and—later—in Suzuki and in Fuji Heavy Industries, Chrysler in Mitsubishi Motors, and Ford in Mazda. Toyota set up a 50:50 production joint venture with General Motors in California in the mid-1980s and launched a Japanese sales network for Volkswagen and Audi vehicles in the early 1990s. European automakers made their first large investments in Japanese automakers in the late 1990s. Renault acquired a controlling stake in Nissan in 1999 and DaimlerChrysler in Mitsubishi Motors in 2000.

Toyota has been the chief mover in equity investments among Japanese automakers. It increased its long-standing equity holdings in the small-car manufacturer Daihatsu and the truck and bus manufacturer Hino incrementally and secured a majority stake in Daihatsu in 1998 and in Hino in 2001. A 2005 investment made Toyota the largest investor in Fuji Heavy Industries (Subaru), and the two companies promptly announced plans for developing and producing vehicles jointly in the United States and in Japan.

The evolving pattern of the Japanese automakers' participation in cross-border alliances has reflected the changing self-awareness of organizational capability. Mazda and Mitsubishi Motors, along with the truck and bus maker Isuzu, embraced Big Three investors in the 1970s. Each of the three took that step out of concern that their financial position was too weak and their production volume too small to remain viable.

In the 1980s, the international competitiveness of the Japanese automakers' organizational capability in manufacturing became inescapably apparent, and U.S. and European automakers moved to secure Japanese know-how in integrated manufacturing systems. That occasioned a new round of strategic collaborations with the Japanese, now regarded as manufacturers to be reckoned with.

Some of Japan's automakers stumbled financially after the collapse of the nation's economic bubble at the outset of the 1990s. Their difficulties stemmed largely from strategic errors, as we have seen, and not from any fundamental weakening of their organizational capability in manufacturing. But whatever the cause, their weakened condition occasioned management changes in which world-class foreign executives took the helm. The most famous example was the turnaround engineered by

Carlos Ghosn at Nissan after Renault acquired control there. Ford's Henry Wallace, meanwhile, preceded Ghosn in Japan by three years and oversaw sweeping changes for the better at Mazda as the first foreign president of a Japanese automaker.

Let us note that a foreign president at the helm signifies as much interest in obtaining insight into organizational capability as in exerting control. Both Renault and Ford secured control over their Japanese partners through large minority stakes, and both Nissan and Mazda have remained highly autonomous and have retained their traditional and highly regarded approaches to capability building. The foreign investors have gone out of their way to learn from and emulate those Japanese approaches. Renault, especially, has worked hard and well to assimilate important elements of Nissan's manufacturing expertise, product technology, and R&D management. It has strengthened Nissan, meanwhile, by infusing the Japanese company with new kinds of competence in strategic planning.

Automakers can remain vigorous platforms for autonomous learning and capability building even after another automaker has acquired all or most of their equity. We have seen that happen at Audi after its acquisition by Volkswagen and at Volvo and Jaguar after their acquisition by Ford. The implicit lesson is that the value of an acquisition hinges greatly on honoring the autonomy of the acquired company and thereby retaining the pride, motivation, and competence essential to its capability building. The vitality of the global automobile industry hinges more on the number of autonomous capability-building platforms—regardless of ownership—than on the number of financially independent companies.

The compatibility of cooperation and competition

Competition among automakers in the marketplace unfolds in the realm of surface competitiveness. Automakers strive to outdo one another in winning customers through such criteria as product performance, styling, reliability, service, pricing, and advertising. Back home in their factories, in their R&D laboratories, and in their marketing and other operations, the automakers compete in regard to deep competitiveness—the organizational capability in creating design information and in transferring that information to products and through the products to customers.

Cooperation can and does reinforce automakers' competitiveness in every facet of surface and deep competitiveness. But for every facet of competitiveness where automakers cooperate, countless more facets remain where the automakers continue to compete aggressively. That is why Adam Smith need not have worried about the global automobile industry descending into collusive oligarchy. At least in the automobile industry, cooperation has served to stimulate, rather than diminish, competition.

Automakers have increased their overall competitiveness by selectively redressing their weaknesses through cooperation. That cooperation has stimulated competition most in the numerous instances where automakers have cooperated in capability building—deep competitiveness—while continuing to compete furiously in pricing and in other facets of surface competitiveness.

Consumers benefit as cooperation reduces the disparities among automakers in deep competitiveness and enables the automakers to offer more-distinctive, more-appealing products. Consumers also benefit as cooperation offers a stay of execution and enables severely weakened automakers to regain their competitive footing. Cooperation, in other words, helps maintain diversity and prevent anticompetitive concentration in the automobile industry.

Automakers of any size or nationality are eligible to participate in capability-reinforcing cooperation with other automakers. Cooperation is a reciprocal undertaking, however, and each participant needs to bring something of value to the table. Some minimal level of independent capability-building competence is the ante, the price of admission. Cooperation is a supplement, not an alternative, to continuing, internal progress in capability building.

7 The Chasers and the Chased

Managements at the U.S. and European automakers finally recognized the crucial role of organizational capability in the competitiveness of the Japanese automakers, and competition in capability building escalated as a result. Some of the U.S. and European automakers began to overcome the competitiveness gap with the Japanese in the 1990s.

Since manufacturing capability at the Japanese automakers had evolved as an emergent process, the resultant manufacturing systems contained a lot of historical baggage that was no longer essential to the systems' functionality. The Americans and Europeans, on the outside looking in, enjoyed an objective perspective on the Japanese production systems. That gave them a useful vantage in identifying what contributed to functionality—and what didn't—in those systems. Their reproductions of the Japanese systems, though inevitably imperfect, were more pure than the originals in the functionality of the constituent elements.

The Japanese automakers responded to the U.S. and European challenge by identifying chinks in their own armor. They discovered a lot of waste, especially in their vehicle design standards. Quality and complexity in their vehicles had reached absurd levels—far beyond anything that consumers would ever notice, much less seek actively.

Excessive quality and complexity had resulted from the inherently beneath-the-surface activity of capability building. Unable to monitor each other's progress in capability building, the Japanese automakers—in the paranoia of competition—built to excess, at least in regard to design capability. Their preoccupation with customer satisfaction—or at least their approach to satisfying customers—was also part of the problem: the automakers employed comprehensive checklists of things they had learned that customers didn't like. They worked scrupulously and successfully to avoid triggering any of the dislikes on their checklists. But in the process, they ended up with specifications that were—in the aggregate—more than any customer really wanted.

FIGURE 7-1

Comparative Performance of Vehicle Assembly Plants in Productivity and Quality

Assembly productivity
Person-hours/vehicle

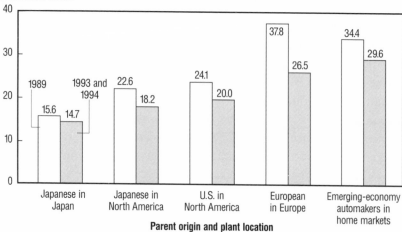

Parent origin and plant location

Manufacturing quality
Defects/100 vehicles

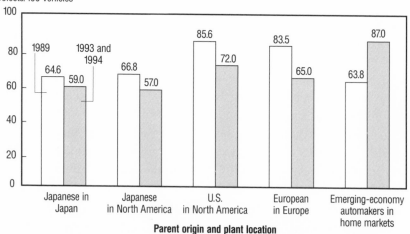

Parent origin and plant location

The data represented in the two graphs pertains to plants covered in both the 1989 and the 1993–1994 surveys by the International Motor Vehicle Program. In regard to productivity, the graph presents data from questionnaire responses provided by the automakers, adjusted for range of work, absenteeism, model size, and other factors. In regard to quality, the graph presents data extracted from study findings published by J.D. Power and Associates.

Source: T. Fujimoto and A. Takeishi (2003), based on findings by MacDuffie et al. at the University of Pennsylvania in surveys conducted under the International Motor Vehicle Program

Another cause of excessive quality and complexity was the influence of the powerful product managers. The sweeping authority of those managers was clearly valuable in maximizing product integrity, but it entailed the danger of overloading models with unique specifications. Each product manager naturally wanted to place a personal imprint on "his" car. That sometimes meant demanding newly developed components for functions where existing items would have served perfectly well.

1. Catching Up with the Japanese

By the mid-1990s, the U.S. and European automakers had greatly narrowed the Japanese automakers' lead in manufacturing cost, assembly productivity, manufacturing quality, development lead time, and other competitive criteria. That is amply evident in the abundant accumulation of pertinent data that is available on this subject. When the yen appreciated against the dollar in the mid-1990s, the United States was basically cost competitive with Japan in automobile manufacturing. The reasons for that parity are clear: the structural upward shift in the valuation of the yen that began with the Plaza Accord of 1985, the slowing of the rise in productivity at the Japanese automakers, the American absorption of Japanese management principles through the Japanese automakers' U.S. plants and through corporate collaborations, and independent efforts by the U.S. automakers to improve their operations. Similar improvement occurred at the European automakers.

The International Motor Vehicle Program documented unmistakable progress at European and U.S. automakers in catching up with the Japanese automakers (fig. 7-1). In assembly productivity, the Europeans' average person-hours per vehicle had declined to 27 in the program's second survey, in 1993 and 1994, from 38 in the first survey, in 1989. The same indicator at the U.S. automakers had declined to 20, from 24. At the Japanese automakers' vehicle plants in Japan, it declined only slightly, to 15, from 16. In manufacturing quality, the number of defects per vehicle had declined to 65, from 84, at the European automakers; to 72, from 86, at the U.S. automakers; and to 59, from 65, at the Japanese automakers's vehicle plants in Japan.

A Harvard-based international survey in which the author participated found equally impressive improvement in R&D productivity at the

FIGURE 7-2

International Comparison of Change from the 1980s to the 1990s in Indicators of Organizational Capability in Product Development

	Japan	U.S.A.	Europe	Average
Development projects	12→8	6→5	11→12	29→25
Lead time (months)	45→55	61→52	59→56	53→55
Productivity (million person-hours)	1.7→2.1	3.4→2.3	2.9→2.8	2.5→2.5
Commodity products in purchasing (percentage of value)	8→6	3→12	6→12	6→10
Share of purchasing based on drawings generated by parts manufacturers and approved by automakers (percentage of value)	62→55	16→30	29→24	40→35
Percentage of purchasing based on drawings furnished to parts manufacturers by automakers (percentage of value)	30→39	81→58	65→64	54→55
Fabrication lead time for first prototype (months)	7→6	12→12	11→9	9→9
Lead time for designing and fabricating dies (months)	14→5	25→20	28→23	22→20
Projects headed by all-powerful product managers (percentage of projects)	17→25	0→20	0→0	7→12
Projects headed by all-powerful or nearly all-powerful product managers (percentage of projects)	83→100	17→100	36→83	52→92
Parts shared among models (% of all parts)	19→28	38→25	30→32	27→29
Index of part complexity	95→68	92→76	83→100	90→85

Source: T. Fujimoto and A. Takeishi (2003)

U.S. automakers (fig. 7-2). The average person-hours devoted to comparable R&D projects at the U.S. automakers had declined to 2.3 million per project in the 1990s, from 3.4 million in the 1980s. Japan's automakers required 2.1 million person-hours per project in comparable projects in the 1990s, so the U.S.-Japanese differential in R&D productivity had become almost negligible. Similarly, the average development lead time, as measured from the start of product planning to the start of preparations for mass production, shrank at the U.S. automakers, to 52 months, from 61, while it lengthened at the Japanese automakers, to 55 months, from 45.

The European automakers made less progress than their U.S. counterparts in narrowing the competitiveness gap with the Japanese in these indicators. Their average person-hours per R&D project declined only to 2.8 million, from 2.9 million, and their development lead time shrank only to 56 months, from 59. Notwithstanding the differing paces of catch-up, a broad convergence in organizational capability was unmistakable in R&D work, as detailed in figure 7-2. Just as unmistakable in that figure, however, is the persistent Japanese edge—though narrowed—in every important indicator of deep competitiveness. Subsequent survey findings suggest, meanwhile, that the Japanese broadened or reasserted their competitive edge, as in development lead time, in the late 1990s.

The process of awakening

Japanese cars asserted compelling competitive strengths in North America several years before they became notably competitive in Europe, and the U.S. automakers began moving several years earlier than the Europeans to incorporate elements of the Japanese production systems. So we will focus on the U.S. automakers in examining the process of awakening that occurred at the U.S. and European automakers. Let us bear in mind, however, that the strategic adjustments by the U.S. automakers were only partly a response to the mounting Japanese challenge. They also addressed other changes in the market environment, such as consumers' dwindling appetite for gas-guzzling behemoths and increasingly stringent government regulations in regard to fuel economy and exhaust emissions. We have mentioned the declining attraction of gas guzzlers in contrast with the growing appeal of fuel-efficient small cars from Japan, but that decline is attributable first and foremost to a basic change in the market conditions: the surging cost of gasoline at the fuel pump.

By the mid-1970s, the U.S. automakers had begun downsizing their bread-and-butter big cars and had begun developing compacts. Their basic strategy continued to center, however, on basically big cars, which offered bigger profit margins.

The U.S. Congress mandated improvements in fuel economy by enacting, in 1975, the Corporate Average Fuel Economy (CAFE) regulations. Those regulations specified minimal levels for the average fuel economy of the vehicles produced by each automaker in North America, they imposed graduated financial penalties on automakers for any shortfall, and they rose annually. The U.S. automakers responded by tweaking their models just enough to meet the CAFE regulations each year while maintaining predominantly large-car fleets.

Things changed abruptly for the Big Three after the second oil crisis, in 1979. The market for big, rear-wheel-drive gas guzzlers imploded. Unit demand for those cars halved overnight. Demand for fuel-efficient small cars, including Japanese imports, grew only slowly, but small cars' market share increased greatly on account of the debacle at the large end of the market.

Management at General Motors resolved to transform the company into a leading supplier of small cars. It established a target of increasing small-car sales to more than one-half of the company's unit sales of passenger cars by 1985, and it invested prodigiously in expanding production capacity for small and fuel-efficient front-wheel-drive models. It funded that investment by promoting high-priced small cars. That stratagem benefited from the artificially inflated prices engendered by the "voluntary" export restraint that Japan's automakers undertook in 1981.

The people at General Motors and at the other U.S. automakers grievously underestimated the competitive strength of the Japanese small cars. Even a lot of people at the Japanese automakers were blind to the fundamental competitiveness of their products. They were in awe of the vast financial resources of the Big Three. The Japanese automakers wouldn't stand a chance, they assumed, if the Big Three got serious about making small cars.

Japanese cars continued to sell well even after a jolting, upward revaluation of the yen against the dollar. Denizens of Detroit sensed that the Japanese automakers' competitive edge was rooted in something bigger than mere wage differentials. Survey findings from such authoritative third parties as J.D. Power and Associates provided convincing statistical evidence of Japanese strengths in quality, as well as cost.

Bosses at the Big Three began to recognize the deep competitiveness that the Japanese had built in such criteria as productivity and quality. And they began to perceive that deep competitiveness in the context of organizational capability in support of integrated manufacturing systems. Simply investing in small-car production capacity, they began to see, was an inadequate response to the challenge at hand.

Acknowledgement of Japanese competitiveness came slowly and grudgingly. Even after the Japanese automakers' edge in manufacturing productivity and in manufacturing quality became undeniable, people at the Big Three and elsewhere failed—or refused—to notice their strengths in development productivity and in product design. A survey conducted in the late 1980s by Kim Clark, then the dean of the Harvard Business School, and the author made those strengths harder to miss. The survey findings documented a Japanese edge in development productivity and in development lead time. Ever so gradually, people realized that catching up with the Japanese would require a complete reworking of the Big Three's basic manufacturing capabilities. That was the beginning of international competition in capability building in the automobile industry.

Learning to be lean

Diverse findings about Japanese strengths in automobiles highlighted the futility of focusing on any single element of competitiveness—development, production, sales, or whatever. A meaningful understanding of competitiveness, people discovered, would require a comprehensive grasp of the overall systems employed by automakers. That discovery gave rise to the International Motor Vehicle Program, and the program's seminal report, published as a book in 1990, characterized the Japanese strengths in a single word: lean.

The best-selling book detailed the success of Toyota and the other Japanese automakers in systematically eliminating waste, raising productivity, and ensuring quality in production and in product development and in purchasing, in sales and service, and in other phases of their operations. It was a wake-up call to manufacturers worldwide: get lean or perish. The book's gripping title, *The Machine That Changed the World*, captured the imagination of researchers everywhere, and the pursuit of "lean" launched a global tidal wave of research into Japanese approaches to manufacturing and, more broadly, to management.

In the late 1980s, Ford was the U.S. automaker that had best absorbed the Japanese lessons of lean production. Ford's vehicle plants in Chicago and Atlanta led the U.S. automobile industry in productivity and in quality. The Ford Taurus, which debuted in 1985, was the first U.S. offspring of quasi-Japanese development by a cross-functional team.

Ford possessed a more nuts-and-bolts manufacturing culture than the other U.S. automakers. Equally important, it lacked the liquidity that General Motors had in the late 1980s to invest heavily in new equipment. That lack, a legacy of financial difficulties in the early 1980s, proved a blessing. It obliged Ford to focus on organizational capability in seeking improvements in competitiveness.

Another advantage that Ford enjoyed in assimilating lean-production concepts was the company's relationship with Japan's Mazda. The Japanese automaker had undergone a serious fiscal crisis of its own in the 1970s, and its recovery program had included adopting Toyota-style approaches to production and to development. It had become an exemplar of lean manufacturing. Mazda was an invaluable source of insight, which Ford, to its credit, used to good effect.

2. Distilling the Message

The emergence we have noted in the development of the Japanese automakers' production systems was a bottom-up affair. Ideas and methods had emerged through ad hoc responses to the challenges presented by domestic competition. To whatever extent management had nursemaided the systems, it had done so by recognizing, adopting, and systematizing contributions that originated in the workplace. The U.S. and European automakers, in contrast, adopted lean manufacturing as a conscious, top-down decision by management. That obliged them to study the Japanese systems analytically; to sort through the presently functional elements and the vestigial, nonfunctional elements; and to codify the systems to convert the tacit knowledge and understanding of the Japanese participants into explicit instructions for North American employees.

As latecomers to lean manufacturing, the U.S. and European automakers enjoyed the advantage of learning from the experience of Japan's lean pioneers. Cultural, social, and even geographical differences surely prevented them from adopting or, sometimes, even noticing some elements of the Japanese version of lean manufacturing. The majority of Toyota's first-tier suppliers, to cite just one example, maintain plants in close proximity to Toyota's vehicle plants. Maintaining just-in-time delivery schedules is far easier for them than for U.S. suppliers that contend with transcontinental logistics.

On the other hand, the latecomer's privilege of analyzing pioneering competitors' practices objectively and of distilling the essential elements of those systems offered important advantages. It enabled the U.S. and European automakers to leapfrog a lot of the trial and error that went into creating the Japanese systems. And it surely enabled them to develop new and better ways of doing things in some parts of their systems.

We have already discussed numerous elements of lean production. So let us look at product development, at purchasing, and at quality control in examining how the U.S. and European automakers adopted elements of the Japanese approaches.

Product development

The emulation of Japanese lean practices that began with the Ford Taurus in the 1980s gained momentum in the 1990s. Chrysler, for example, adopted the Japanese "big-room" format in assembling platform teams for developing its principal models. All of the engineers responsible for the principal vehicle functions—power train, body, suspension, etc.—worked together in a single, expansive workplace. That was to break down the factionalism that had frequently impeded progress in product development, to improve communication among participants in product development, and to shorten the time required for developing vehicle models.

Chrysler's new approach to product development contained important input from American Motors and from Honda. The company had acquired American Motors in 1987. Honda, meanwhile, was Chrysler's chief reference for benchmarking in product development. The new approach shortened Chrysler's lead time greatly in product development. New Chrysler models appeared in showrooms only 30 months, on average, after management signed off on the vehicle designs. That was down from 40 months previously, though it was still more time than the Japanese automakers required.

Ironically, Japan's automakers rarely employed the big-room format as Chrysler did. The engineers responsible for different functions often worked concurrently on multiple vehicle development projects, so deploying them physically by development project would be impractical. Only for emergency projects and in other special circumstances did the Japanese automakers put all the functional engineers in the same room. Ordinarily, the functional engineers worked in workplaces with other engineers responsible for the same functions.

People responsible for product development at the Japanese automakers were generally skeptical of Chrysler's approach. They acknowledged the value of that approach in shortening lead time, but they noted that assigning functional engineers directly to product development projects entailed a great deal of redundancy, that it undermined the company's capacity for long-term development in functional technologies, and that it impeded coordination among product development projects. Several of their colleagues, however, expressed more-positive opinions about the Chrysler experiment. Whatever its net benefits, the experiment was a classic example of achieving accelerated results by supercharging elements gleaned from Japanese practices.

Purchasing

U.S. perceptions of Japanese practices were evident in the sterling performance of Thomas Stallkamp in reworking Chrysler's worldwide purchasing operations. His success in reorienting the automaker's supplier relationships vaulted him into the presidency of the company in 1996. Under Stallkamp, Chrysler built a purchasing organization that was the envy of the automobile industry in North America and in Europe. His description of the successful transformation of Chrysler's purchasing matches closely what happened in Japan's automobile industry from the 1950s to the 1970s:

• Increase the percentage of parts purchased from third-party suppliers.
• Increase the percentage of parts design work handled by independent suppliers.
• Reduce the number of first-tier parts suppliers.
• Purchase an increased percentage of parts from first-tier suppliers as integrated assemblies, rather than as individual parts.
• Build a multilevel supply network that encompasses second- and third-tier suppliers, as well as first-tier suppliers.
• Secure the participation of first-tier suppliers in development work on parts for next-generation vehicle models.
• Work with suppliers to find ways to lower their costs rather than unilaterally demanding price reductions.
• Adopt cost-planning methods based on target prices.
• Share knowledge with parts suppliers.
• Step up technical cooperation in every phase of the automaker-supplier relationship.

All of the measures cited by Stallkamp had contributed greatly to strengthening the competitiveness of the Japanese automakers. All of them coincided, meanwhile, with another characteristic Japanese approach: the automakers' much-maligned *keiretsu* practice of maintaining close relationships with basically fixed coteries of closely affiliated suppliers. The affiliation often, though not always, included minority or even majority equity holdings by the automakers in the suppliers. Executives from the automakers served on the boards of directors at core suppliers, and the suppliers devoted priority to their business with a single automaker, though they served their and their main customer's interests by maximizing economies of scale through business with multiple automakers.

Keiretsu relationships are an example of the historical baggage borne by the Japanese automakers, and they are not necessarily essential to the advantages that have accrued from Japanese approaches to purchasing and to supplier management. To be sure, the feudalistic ties that bound the vehicle-assembling lords and their parts-making vassals were useful to the automakers. They were instrumental in securing reliable quantities of quality parts during the Japanese automobile industry's years of rapid growth. And a lot of people in the industry insist that the absolute trust inherent to *keiretsu* relationships remains indispensable in joint development work on core components and systems.

Even granting the historical and possibly continuing value of *keiretsu* ties, we cannot fail to recognize the anticompetitive aspect of favoring affiliated suppliers in awarding purchasing contracts. That negative aspect of *keiretsu* became a competitive albatross when the growth in Japanese vehicle production ceased and the Japanese automakers began globalizing their production and their purchasing in earnest.

Toyota indirectly acknowledged the problem in announcing its Global Optimum Purchasing program in the mid-1990s. The automaker declared that it would henceforth allocate its purchasing contracts to the suppliers that offered the highest quality, the lowest costs, the most interesting product development, and the most reliable delivery in a global context—*irrespective of nationality, corporate size, or track record in business with Toyota.* That seemingly innocuous declaration merely repeated what had long been Toyota's stated policy in purchasing, but it sent a clear and alarming message to Toyota's Japanese suppliers: The era of global competition has arrived, and hometown sentimentality will no longer figure in our purchasing. The declaration was also a sincere invitation to non-Japanese suppliers: If you thought the door to Toyota's purchasing organization was closed, think again. We are seriously interested in competitive products from any source.

In practice, Toyota's Global Optimum Purchasing has taken hold gradually, and the abandonment of *keiretsu* considerations has been less than total. But Toyota has unquestionably taken huge strides in globalizing its purchasing, and accompanying that globalization has been an unprecedented openness in cultivating supplier relationships.

Even more drastic than Toyota's purchasing transformation was the purchasing revolution at Nissan after Renault took control in 1999. Carlos Ghosn sounded the death knell for *keiretsu* there and launched a ruthless purge of uncompetitive suppliers. Nissan has remained a paragon, however, of the purchasing practices described by Chrysler's Stallkamp. It, along with Toyota, has thereby demonstrated that those practices, which originated in Japan, are not inextricably linked to *keiretsu* relationships.

Quality control

Japanese manufacturers' biggest contribution to the evolution of quality control was in making it truly "total." They started with the statistical quality control brought to Japan by Americans after World War II, and they made it better. They did that by putting everyone in every workplace in charge of monitoring and ensuring the quality of the work at hand. That included encouraging everyone to identify opportunities for improvements and empowering people in the workplace to take the initiative in putting ideas for improvements into practice.

The tools for applying total quality control spanned advanced statistical analysis and gritty trial and error in the workplace, led by quality control circles. Companies motivated workers with awards for accomplishments in quality control. Japanese industry established the (W. Edwards) Deming Prize, named for the American who proselytized quality control in postwar Japan. Companies earned—and continue to earn—that prize by achieving distinctive improvements in quality by applying the principles of total quality control. Industrywide organizations worked with quality control experts in academia to identify best practice and to propagate successful methods throughout Japanese industry.

U.S. manufacturers learned from the Japanese and adopted the principles of total quality control under the name total quality management. The name change emphasized the U.S. emphasis on engaging senior management in the task of ensuring high and consistent quality. In 1987, Congress established a U.S. version of the Deming Prize, the Malcolm Baldrige National Quality Award. A panel of government and private-sector adjudicators administers the Baldrige award, which bears the name of a former secretary of commerce. The stated purpose of the award is "to recognize U.S. organizations for their achievements in quality and performance and to raise awareness about the importance of quality and performance excellence as a competitive edge."

Total quality management was more top down in its approach than the Japanese total quality control, and the impressive results that it supported at numerous U.S. manufacturers captured attention in Japan. By the late 1990s, the U.S. nomenclature had become common in Japan as TQM, and Japanese companies had adopted a visibly more top-down approach. The Japan Quality Award, established in 1995 and administered by the nonprofit Japan Productivity Center for Socio-Economic Development, reflects the top-down, strategic orientation of total quality management.

Japanese practitioners of total quality control had focused on improving production processes to prevent product defects. In contrast, total quality management shifted the focus to comprehensive quality as perceived from the perspective of customer satisfaction. It emphasized improvements in the quality of management as the foundation of product quality. And it highlighted the linkage between management strategy and activity in the workplace. Japanese companies had employed so-called policy deployment (*hoshin kanri* in Japanese) to translate overall goals into concrete targets for each workplace team and individual, but the strategic positioning of the overall goals at the top end of policy deployment was frequently inconsistent.

Total quality management also employed more-rigorously statistical approaches to problem solving than had been common in total quality control. Epitomizing the more-sophisticated approaches to statistical analysis was the Six Sigma methodology created at Motorola, which gained fame at Jack Welch's General Electric. In addition, total quality management mobilized cross-functional cooperation in support of quality improvements. Japanese manufacturers had mobilized everyone in their companies in the quest for quality, but the measures for improving processes had tended to take place within the confines of individual workplaces.

We should take note in passing of the International Organization for Standardization's ISO 9000 family of standards for quality management systems. Those standards, which first appeared in 1987, originated in the British Standards Institution's BS 5750. They were yet another step away from the traditional Japanese reliance on internal, workplace initiative. The ISO 9000 standards evinced the characteristically occidental predilection for applying the quantitative yardsticks of third-party guidelines. To the extent that ISO 9000 certification became a condition for doing business with numerous companies, it reinforced corporate competitiveness. But the author is aware of few instances of companies, at least in Japan, that have improved product quality significantly through the process of earning the certification.

3. Capability Building to a Fault

The appreciation of the yen after the Plaza Accord of 1985 exposed the excess that permeated the Japanese automakers' design standards. That excess, manifest in overly complex specifications and in meaninglessly rigorous quality standards, contrasted with the Japanese automakers' leanness in production. It was the result of capability building run amok, and it took several forms; for example, more models and model variations than demand justified, more model-specific parts than were necessary to assert distinct model identities, more-frequent model changes than the market could digest, more features and options per model than customers needed or wanted, sophisticated functions more costly than sticker prices could absorb fully.

Too many model variations

By the early 1990s, concern about the profusion of model variations was widespread in the Japanese automobile industry. Typical of the glut was the product portfolio at a Toyota plant that produced about 60,000 vehicles a month. Nearly half of that output—about 25,000 vehicles—consisted of model variations that each accounted for only a single vehicle per month. That kind of excess entailed the obvious problems of inflated costs in product development and diminished economies of scale in production. It also spawned the problems of bloated inventories of parts, a confusing array of parts alongside the assembly line, an increased risk of attaching the wrong part, heightened complexity in ensuring reliable supplies of replacement parts, and impediments to automation.

The burgeoning diversity of product variations might appear to have been an unavoidable response to the explosive diversity in demand—necessary in the interest of customer satisfaction. However, the immediate source of the demand for all those model variations was not consumers in the marketplace. Rather, it was the car dealers. The dealers placed orders for a dizzying multiversity of products with an eye to promoting them to customers. And the dealers' ordering did not necessarily reflect the minimum range of model variations necessary to "keep the customer satisfied."

That the number of model variations had become excessive seems undeniable, but whether the number of basic models—platforms—was excessive is more difficult to ascertain. The appropriate breadth of an automaker's core model line is a function of fundamental strategic considerations, including overall production volume, target market segments, and basic capacity for flexible manufacturing. We lack sufficient data to render a conclusive judgment on the Japanese automakers' strategies in deploying their basic model lines. The available data suggests, however, that our judgment would vary significantly by automaker. In contrast, the gratuitous over-deployment of model variations afflicted every company in the industry conspicuously.

Too many model-specific parts

The percentage of parts common to multiple models was generally lower at the Japanese automakers in the 1980s than at the U.S. or European automakers. That is a finding of research by the author and colleagues. The percentage of parts in each model common to other models—including the previous generation of the same model—averaged about 20% at the Japanese automakers, 30% at the European automakers, and 40% at the U.S. automakers.

A high percentage of model-specific parts—that is, a low percentage of parts common to multiple models—can be valuable in asserting a strong model identity and in differentiating models advantageously from the competition. The percentage of model-specific parts in the Japanese vehicles was demonstrably higher, however, than anything justifiable under those criteria. An astonishing plethora of parts filled the automakers' catalogs of product specifications while providing no substantive functional or stylistic distinction from other parts. Finding ways to share more parts among models without undermining customer appeal became an especially pressing concern as growth in Japanese vehicle production ceased.

Too frequent model changes

A four-year product cycle for most of the Japanese automakers' principal passenger car models had worked well since the 1960s, but it became untenable in the 1990s. Four-year product cycles gave way to five-year cycles for several Japanese vehicle models, though the shorter cycles remained common for core models. Several considerations forced the lengthening of product cycles. Most notably, the Japanese automakers needed to

- trim costs in vehicle development,
- lighten the burden of work on their development and production engineering personnel,
- give their suppliers more time to recoup the investment made in development parts,
- retain customers better by extending the product life of new cars, and
- alleviate trade frictions by reducing the pressure on the U.S. and European automakers, who were struggling to keep up with the Japanese pace of model changes.

Newly launched models account for a disproportionate share of sales in every market, and their sales weighting is especially large in Japan. So maintaining a young model line is indispensable in the Japanese market. No automaker could afford to lengthen its product cycle dramatically, but stretching out the cycle a year or two for selected models was at least partly effective in addressing the above considerations.

Too much functionality and quality

The Japanese automakers laded their cars in the 1980s with embarrassing loads of superfluous features and functions. Even a lot of the items that were essentially useful were unnecessarily complex in their design and materials. That lading frequently occurred through equipping mid-priced and entry-level models with features and functions developed originally for premium-grade models. Along with making the ostensibly affordable models unnecessarily expensive, that diluted the cachet associated with the high-end models. Sales of several models suffered as a result when Japan's bubble economy burst at the outset of the 1990s.

That said, let us be wary of jumping to conclusions about specifications that might seem excessive at first glance. The Japanese automakers, for example, tended to employ bolts engineered especially for specified applications in their vehicles, whereas the U.S. automakers were more likely to opt for general-purpose bolts. Specially configured bolts are more expensive, of course, than general-purpose bolts, and any advantages that they offer might not be readily apparent. The general-purpose bolts might perform as well as the specially configured bolt for the first few years of vehicle life, but the parts that they secure might become more prone to rattling after a few years.

Bolt selection is an admittedly unexciting but ever-so-real example of an engineering difference that affects market pricing. That is evident in North American survey findings about used-car prices in the 1990s. Locally produced Honda Accords and Toyota Camrys retained more than 50% of their sticker price as three-year-old used cars, whereas comparable models from the U.S. automakers retained less than 40% of their original price. That differential is attributable at least partly to exactly the kind of engineering seen in our example of bolt selection. Anticipated resale value figures mightily in new-car pricing in North America, so even design specifications whose usefulness only becomes apparent over the long term can contribute to new-car value. Strong resale value was the salvation of the Japanese automakers in North America when the yen appreciated anew in the 1990s.

Precisely quantifying the degree of over-engineering that occurred in the 1980s is impossible. For example, using three bolts to secure a part where two would suffice might offer some small advantage, and the value of that advantage depends on product positioning. Only the designers and engineers who determine the specifications can judge, even in retrospect, what was true to their product concept and strategy. Anecdotal evidence of the excesses of the era is, however, readily available. Comments by a design engineer at a German automaker in a 1988 interview with the author are notably illuminating.

The engineer mentioned his company's findings from reverse engineering the leading mass-market vehicles from German and Japanese automakers. He confided that Japanese models were about $500 more costly per car in their construction than comparable German models. The Japanese automakers reported achieving big cost reductions in the early 1990s through value analysis activities (cost-saving design improvements in models already in mass production) and value engineering activities (cost-saving improvements in the development stage). The amounts of those reported cost savings provide after-the-fact confirmation of the engineering excesses of the 1980s.

4. Simplifying Design

Restoring cost competitiveness by redressing the sins of over-engineering was the biggest and the largely unreported story of Japanese manufacturing in the 1990s. Continual, incremental improvements in the production workplace had long been the chief driver in cost-reduction activities at the Japanese automakers. After decades of generating impressive cumulative benefits, however, those improvements were inevitably subject to the law of diminishing returns. Seeking a quantum leap in cost reductions, the automakers turned their eyes to product design. Their competitive restoration centered on successful measures for simplifying product specifications, and those measures continue in the opening decade of the 21st century.

The results have been genuinely spectacular. Return on sales at the Japanese automakers overall turned upward after 1993. That upturn occurred amid the punishing appreciation of the yen—a dollar bought little more than ¥80 in spring 1995—and it resulted from the automakers' progress in cost-cutting capability building. The 1990s were the "lost

FIGURE 7-3
Factors in Operating Income at Toyota (¥ billion)

	1993	1994	1995	1996	1997	1998	1999	2000	2001
Currency exchange rates	−160.0	−80.0	−20.0	+240.0	+100.0	+100.0	−430.0	−170.0	−410.0
Unit sales volume and selling prices	−70.0	+70.0	−50.0	+60.0	−140.0	−110.0	+220.0	+210.0	−90.0
Cost reductions*	+150.0	+150.0	+130.0	+110.0	+70.0	+120.0	+150.0	+190.0	+260.0
Depreciation, other**	+53.1	−9.9	−31.6	−128.2	+13.3	−153.2	+61.0	−136.4	−326.7
Change in operating income	−26.9	+130.1	+28.4	+281.8	+43.3	−43.2	+1.0	+93.6	+253.3

* Cost savings achieved through improvements in product designs, production processes, and logistics.
** Including R&D expenses and personnel expenses, as well as depreciation and amortization.
Source: Materials released by Toyota

decade" of essentially zero expansion for the Japanese economy, but the nation's automakers were a shining exception.

Toyota slashed its costs an average of more than ¥120 billion a year during the 1990s (fig. 7-3). That cost cutting offset the frequently adverse effect of fluctuations in the valuation of the yen, and Toyota achieved nearly 80% of its cost savings by rationalizing product designs: sharing more parts among models, reducing the number of model variations, making vehicles easier to build. Supplementing the cost savings of design rationalization were cost reductions through continuing improvements in production processes and improvements in logistics. Japan's other automakers achieved similar progress in slashing costs. Here, we will take a closer look at successful efforts in sharing parts among models and in consolidating vehicle platforms. Bear in mind that other efforts, such as eliminating unnecessary complexity in vehicle designs, were equally important in cutting costs.

Sharing parts among models

Survey findings by the author and colleagues reveal a sharp decline in the percentage of model-specific parts in Japanese vehicle models. That percentage in selected models had declined to about 60% in the late 1990s, from about 80% in the late 1980s. Toyota and Nissan announced plans in the early 1990s for wholesale reductions in the variety of parts that they handled, and they moved aggressively in fulfilling those plans. Honda was equally aggressive. Shared parts accounted for about 50% of the content of Honda's remodeled Accord that went on sale in 1993 and of its Odyssey minivan, which debuted in 1995.

Something well worth repeating here is the importance of maintaining a distinctive character for each model even while reducing reliance on model-specific parts. The distinctiveness—and, thus, the competitiveness—of some models suffered perceptibly from the increase in parts sharing. But for the most part, Japan's automakers were strikingly successful in finding ways to share parts without diluting product identity.

Consolidating platforms

The cost benefits of sharing parts are especially large when automakers adopt common or nearly common platforms for different models. Building a new model on an existing platform can reduce capital spending up to one-half. It also reduces costs by decreasing the amount of development testing needed and the number of prototypes required, and it lops several months off of the lead time for product development.

Japan's automakers had expanded their platform portfolios steadily up to the 1980s. They did that to optimize the platform for each model. When circumstances forced them to consolidate platforms in the mid-1990s, they found new ways to maintain distinctive model identities. An interesting example is the case of Fuji Heavy Industries (Subaru), the smallest mass-production automaker in Japan.

Fuji adopted a single platform—broadly defined—for all its models as part of a corporate recovery program in the 1990s. Yet its products remained distinctive and popular, especially its flagship model, the Legacy. Fuji ranked high among Japan's automakers in brand value at the end of the decade. Its financial recovery, too, was successful, and the company boasted the highest return on equity among all the Japanese automakers in 2000. Fuji's success is proof positive that even smallish automakers can assert a competitive presence in the marketplace through capability building.

A case study in intelligent compromise in design: Mazda's MX-5

A fascinating exception to the 1980s trend of excess in vehicle design and specifications was Mazda's MX-5 (also known as the Miata in North America; sold in Japan as the Eunos Roadster). The now-legendary MX-5 debuted in 1989 as a revival of the classic British sports car. But it was almost stillborn. The development project for the MX-5 survived the hatchet from senior management at least once. A cabal of committed designers and engineers reportedly kept the project alive by taking it underground.

Even with the subsequent blessing of management, the MX-5 development project was a hand-to-mouth undertaking. Its mandate was to create a car that would be profitable at a sales volume of 50,000 units a year. To restrain costs, the project team was extraordinarily small—fewer than 100 full-time in-house participants, supplemented by parts suppliers' engineers. Of course, the team needed to rely extensively on off-the-shelf parts and on inexpensive materials. The vehicle would be available with but a single body type.

Mazda bent its design standards and testing standards to accommodate the bare-bones development project. The project team skimped wherever possible. On the other hand, it was uncompromising in regard to anything that would affect the MX-5's performance and handling. Everyone on the team was determined to make the most of the new model as a genuine sports car. The chief luxury was a newly developed platform. Minimizing weight was essential, meanwhile, so the team chose aluminum over the less-expensive steel for the hood.

Heading the development effort was a powerful product manager who had the final say in every phase of the project. His strong leadership and the prompt decision making that it made possible were instrumental in allocating scarce resources where they were most needed.

The development team fulfilled its cost mandate, and the MX-5 thus contributed handsomely to Mazda's earnings at its peak sales volume of nearly 100,000 units. It generated unusually steady sales for a sports car and has continued to fortify Mazda's sales performance. Automotive journalists and other professionals loved the car as much as consumers did. Mazda had proved that new kinds of capability building could produce satisfied customers while simplifying design and lowering costs. Its MX-5 was, in that sense, ahead of its time—a harbinger of what lay in store for the entire industry.

8 The Never-Ending Story of Capability-Building Competition

The author has sought in this book to demonstrate that
- the Japanese automakers accumulated unique strengths in the course of building highly integrated production systems;
- the integral architecture of the automobile amplified the efficacy of those strengths in asserting international competitiveness;
- the Japanese automakers' organizational capability in manufacturing arose through an emergent process and was thus difficult to emulate or even, initially, to detect;
- trade frictions and strategic alliances received a lot of attention in the last quarter of the 20th century but were basically a sideshow in the larger scheme of competition in the automobile industry—automakers' individual progress in capability building remained the chief competitive dynamic in the industry;
- managements at the U.S. and European automakers finally recognized the significance of the Japanese automakers' organizational capability in manufacturing and set to work on distilling what they perceived to be the essential elements of the Japanese production systems; and
- the Japanese responded to the U.S. and European challenge by redressing the product excesses that had resulted from the excessive accumulation of capability.

In this concluding chapter, we will examine the pattern of capability-building competition in the 21st century.

1. The More Things Change...

Numerous observers in the 1990s predicted that information technology would rewrite the ground rules for competition in the automobile industry. Advances in information technology have unquestionably affected automobile manufacturing hugely. But instead of establishing some new

FIGURE 8-1

Problem-Solving Curves and Development Lead Time

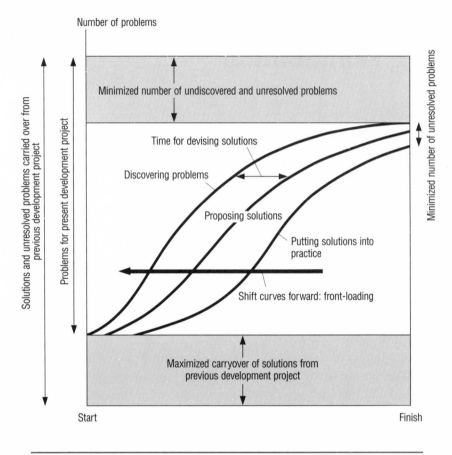

mode of competition, information technology has reinforced the long-standing pattern of competition in capability building. It has simply joined other weapons in the automakers' arsenals for asserting deep competitiveness. Let's examine the role of information technology in a hotly contested phase of capability building in the automobile industry: shortening lead times in product development.

Front-loading

Product development in the automobile industry unfolds through cycles of identifying and solving problems. Amassing skills and resources for identifying and solving problems earlier and more comprehensively is a big part of capability building in product development. So-called front-loading is an especially important emphasis. Automakers use that term in reference to structurally accelerated development schedules. That acceleration is a matter of increasing the density of problem-solving activity in the early stages of development work and reducing the density of that activity in the late stages (fig. 8-1).

Front-loading illuminates problems during "front-end" work, such as preparing design drawings, when adjustments can be made quickly and easily, and helps avoid problems during subsequent work, such as fabricating prototypes, when adjustments are time-consuming and costly. The late stages of vehicle development coincide with preparations for mass production, and minimizing the occurrence of problems in those stages is crucial to achieving smooth product launches. Of course, front-loading also contributes to shortening overall lead times in product development.

Front-loading is a combination of solving problems common to multiple vehicle models and solving problems unique to the model at hand. The former kind of problem solving hinges on organizational memory: remembering the problems that arose in previous development projects and taking steps to address them even earlier the next time. The latter depends on envisioning ever earlier in development how a vehicle's numerous parts and systems will interact in the complete vehicle.

Both kinds of problem solving benefit hugely from applying the digital processing of information technology. Computerization provides storage and referencing support for organizational memory. Three-dimensional rendering with computer graphics, meanwhile, has allowed for identifying and solving problems that formerly lay unnoticed until the physical prototyping stage. Early-stage problem solving with highly accurate 3-D images has reduced the number of times that automakers and parts makers need to fabricate, evaluate, and modify prototypes. It has even eliminated physical prototyping altogether in some development work.

Front-loading is the right way—the sustainable way—to shorten development lead time. It is sustainable because it shifts forward the ascending curves in figure 8-1: curves that represent the unfolding of the work of detecting problems, devising solutions, and putting the solutions to work. Shifting those curves forward entails creative tension, but that tension is a far cry from the outright stress that accompanies unilateral demands from management to "Move faster!" Forcing the acceleration of development projects by simply cracking the whip can work occasionally, but the resultant strain typically shows up somewhere or another, such as in quality problems after cars are in production. In contrast, structurally redeploying resources—problem-solving resources—toward the front end of development schedules speeds development without producing undue strain.

Development resources span every phase of an automaker's technological portfolio, and the Japanese automakers' organizational capability in highly integrated production systems has given them an edge in seamless front-loading. Information technology has furnished convincing, if backhanded, proof of the value of that capability in speeding development. Digital processing and storage, as we have seen, are invaluable in front-loading, and the U.S. and European automakers invested in supercomputers and other digital apparatuses for computer-aided design and engineering earlier and more heavily than the Japanese automakers. Yet the Japanese automakers have led the industry in shortening lead time.

Japan's automakers were already a lot faster than their U.S. and European counterparts in developing passenger cars in the early 1990s. Their average time to the showroom after settling on a basic design was about 30 months, compared with about 40 months for the Americans and Europeans. By the end of the decade, the Japanese had chopped that lead time to 20 months or less. They had mobilized all pertinent divisions to achieve greater perfection in their early-stage product drawings. That had included coming to terms about what went wrong in recent projects and about how to avoid similar problems the next time around; using computer-aided engineering to link design data directly to the fabrication of tools and dies and to other phases of preparations for mass production; and using "rapid-prototyping" technology to link design data directly to equipment for fabricating the prototypes of parts automatically.

The Japanese automakers' organizational capability enabled them to coordinate all that activity among divisions smoothly and to thereby shift forward the entire front end of their development work. Information technology had merely raised the stakes and amplified the importance of traditional strengths in capability building.

2. New Kinds of Cars, New Ways of Making Cars

Advances in information technology have thus reinforced, rather than negated, the importance of traditional capability building in the automobile industry. Other developments, however, could—theoretically—marginalize hard-won strengths in organizational capability. A revolution in vehicle technology could reshape the competitive criteria for automakers. A revolution in production systems could be equally disruptive. We will take a look at potentially disruptive technologies and see why the author expects capability building in integral-architecture manufacturing to define automakers' competitiveness for the foreseeable future.

Vehicle technologies

The automobile bears the "original sin" of causing pollution, global warming, resource depletion, traffic accidents, noise, and other evils too numerous to name. Efforts to promote motor transport will always need to include measures for visibly ameliorating those evils. Conceivably, someone could achieve a technological breakthrough that would eliminate or largely eliminate one or more of those evils. Such a breakthrough could mean fundamental changes in the way vehicles operate. It could render some of the leading automakers' core strengths obsolete. With all due respect to accidents, noise, and other vehicular vices, noxious emissions and fuel economy receive by far the most attention in regard to hoped-for dramatic breakthroughs. No such breakthroughs are visible on the horizon, though—at least not from the vantage point of the author.

Fuel-cell vehicles remain prohibitively expensive, and their energy-conversion efficiency is presently not significantly higher than that of hybrid cars already in mass production. Meanwhile, the energy expended and carbon dioxide emitted in producing and distributing their hydrogen fuel largely offsets their appeal in regard to reducing energy consumption and carbon dioxide emissions. Battery-powered electric vehicles remain disappointing in regard to cost, performance, and net energy savings. Other alternative fuels and their sources, such as natural gas and biomass, presumably warrant continuing, careful attention. But none of them exhibit any compelling advantage over the well-established fuel regimes of gasoline and diesel.

Improving gasoline and diesel power train systems—including hybrid systems—will surely be the most effective way to increase energy efficiency and reduce emissions for the time being. A growing diversity of power train systems will render service on the world's streets and highways, but gasoline and diesel systems will undoubtedly remain preeminent for the foreseeable future.

Another revolution that could revalue automakers' deep competitiveness would be a shift to an open-architecture form of modular product architecture. As we have seen, integral product architecture—the architecture of rubbing things together—has played to the Japanese automakers' strengths in organizational capability. Those strengths are far less important in product sectors where open modular architecture prevails. A wholesale shift to battery-powered electric cars, for instance, could conceivably usher in a generation of "plug-and-play" vehicle architecture. That kind of dramatic shift in power train technologies is highly unlikely, however, in the short and medium term. Longer-term possibilities are less predictable. They are subject to such variables as the timing of the impending decline in global production of crude oil and the pace of the surge under way in vehicle demand in China, India, and other newly emerging economies.

Advances in software for integrating the electronic control of vehicle functions could also spur momentum toward open product architecture. Highly integrated software control would diminish the importance of rubbing things together to optimize the interaction of mechanical components and systems. It could open the door to expanded use of commodity, industry-standard components in automobiles.

Another wildcard in the outlook for integral product architecture is Chinese manufacturing. China's manufacturers have proved masters at dissecting foreign products, such as washing machines, televisions, and even automobiles, and at recreating them with locally obtained parts. They produce low-cost, knockoff versions of Japanese passenger cars, for example, with combinations of commodity components and independently designed parts. That kind of vehicle production amounts to replacing the integral architecture of the original models with open modular architecture, and it could prove competitive at the low end of the price spectrum in other nations, too. China's knockoff passenger cars are conspicuously inferior to the originals, though, in product integrity. Their quality and performance are unlikely to appeal to upwardly mobile consumers whose rising income levels make better cars affordable.

Japan's automakers became internationally competitive through capability building in integral-architecture manufacturing. They can ill afford to ignore the potential challenge from open modular architecture. They need to be prepared to cope with potentially disruptive trends in product technology. On the other hand, integral architecture seems certain to remain dominant in passenger cars for the time being. Automakers of any nationality will do well to continue to concentrate on capability building in rubbing things together.

Production systems

The Japanese automakers' success has occasioned a conceptual convergence in approaches to passenger car manufacturing. The oft-predicted convergence in production systems has not occurred, however, and the world's automakers continue to employ widely divergent production formats even as they all adopt principles of lean production.

Leveled production—handling multiple product specifications on the same production line and distributing the production of different model variations evenly—remains a hallmark of Toyota manufacturing. Some small-car plants in Europe adhere, however, to the traditional practice of producing each model variation in large lots. Those plants tend to employ larger production lines than are common in Japan, and their undifferentiated product mix presents less need for deploying multiskilled workers and continually adjusting the range of tasks that each worker handles. That approach, similar to Henry Ford's, works well as long as the automakers can continue selling their vehicles in large volumes.

Even in Japan, automakers employ diverse manufacturing formats. Honda, for example, is more amenable than Toyota to producing vehicles of the same basic specifications in batches, and it is just as competitive as its larger rival in manufacturing efficiency. Nissan, meanwhile, has developed yet another approach, which is also highly competitive.

An interesting departure from the Ford-Toyota tradition of assembly line production took place in Sweden in the early 1990s. Volvo abandoned the conveyor line at its Uddevalla Plant. Instead, it put small teams of workers in charge of assembling complete automobiles. The experiment addressed a perceived shortcoming of factory work that has concerned observers since the dawn of the Industrial Revolution: that the work is dehumanizing. Mass production notoriously displaced the artisanship of creating products in accordance with the individual sensibility of the craftsperson. It replaced that work with specialization in which workers performed a narrow range of repetitive tasks all day long. Volvo sought to "rehumanize" work by giving workers the chance to take charge of crafting entire products. The Uddevalla format proved uncompetitive, and Volvo ended up selling the plant. But the automaker retained that production format for some kinds of low-volume specialty vehicles, such as limousines and emergency vehicles.

The diversity in manufacturing formats is less inconsistent with a conceptual convergence than it might appear at first glance. Witness the examples of two Toyota subsidiaries: Kanto Auto Works, which assembles low-volume vehicle models for Toyota, and Hino Motors, which produces medium- and heavy-duty trucks under the Hino name, as well as assembling smaller vehicles under the Toyota name.

Kanto Auto Works' product portfolio includes the Century, a large luxury car marketed mainly in Japan as chauffeured transport for executives. It produces that model with small teams of workers who assemble entire vehicles, much like the teams at Volvo's Uddevalla Plant. The teams take hours per vehicle for the assembly work, and Kanto Auto Works turns out just a few score Centurys per month.

Hino Motors' production of heavy-duty trucks is also a far cry from the high-paced production at Toyota's main vehicle plants. The company has even separated the work of selecting and removing parts from stock and the work of attaching them to the vehicles. At a large-volume Toyota plant, arraying parts along the production line streamlines work. But the much-slower pace of truck assembly at Hino makes that unnecessary. Hino's slow-moving assembly line is also suggestive of the Uddevalla Plant, where workers built vehicles on stationary mounts. A former Hino president told the author that management was considering assembling trucks on stationary mounts, à la Volvo.

We can safely assume that Kanto Auto Works and Hino hew to Toyota policy in manufacturing practices. They demonstrate the latitude within the Toyota Production System for accommodating special circumstances. Both examples are entirely consistent with the principles of lean manufacturing. They are simply extreme instances of using human resources efficiently by deploying multiskilled workers to handle multiple tasks. Kanto Auto Works and Hino, in other words, have adopted quintessentially lean responses to small production volumes. Let us also note in passing the remarkable amalgams of artisanship and integrated production that their manufacturing formats represent.

If companies in the Toyota Group can apply the same basic principles of lean production in such widely differing formats, we should hardly be surprised to find automakers of different nationalities applying those principles in an even-greater diversity of formats. Competition in pricing, styling, performance, and other elements of surface competitiveness enforces a stunning conformity in products. In contrast, competition in capability building—deep competitiveness—encourages a vibrant diversity in approaches to making cars.

The world's automakers, for all their diversity in production formats, face common issues, and they have adopted similar responses to those issues. Here are some of the chief examples.

Shorter assembly lines

Vehicle assembly lines are getting shorter. That is a result of the parallel evolution in product architecture and in process architecture, and the operative principle here is modularization. Preassembling parts in functionally or structurally stand-alone modules has been part of the recent architectural evolution of automobiles. That trend reflects a principle articulated famously by the American polymath Herbert Simon, a 1978 Nobel laureate in economics. Simon demonstrated that in complex systems—like automobiles—bundling components in large, functionally autonomous or structurally stable modules maximizes efficiency and quality. Here is how modularization is helping to shorten automakers' assembly lines.

Let us compare newly built assembly lines for producing passenger cars at the rate of around one per minute. The author estimates that the average line of that kind is about 40% shorter today than in the 1980s. Some

15 or 20 years ago, the line would comprise about 200 processes. A comparable line today typically consists of only about 120 processes.

All other things being equal, shorter assembly lines mean that people on the lines assemble vehicles from fewer parts. More assembly work takes place, that is, before the parts reach the main assembly lines. Automakers put their cars together, as Simon recommended, from highly integrated subassemblies: cockpit modules that encompass instrument panels, air conditioner ducts, center consoles, and other interior items; doors that practically snap into place; engine and transmission units that require little more than bolting into vehicles.

The preassembly work takes place on increasingly longer subassembly lines. Shifting assembly work to subassembly lines simplifies vehicle assembly greatly. It also helps achieve a more-even distribution of work on the vehicle lines, since preassembly eliminates a lot of troublesome work prone to bottlenecks. It frequently is an opportunity for automating work, since automated equipment is easier to install away from the vehicle lines.

In Japan, the subassembly lines are usually alongside the main assembly lines inside the vehicle plants. Lowering costs by outsourcing subassembly work to lower-wage suppliers has been a motivation for modularization in other nations. But cost is less of a consideration in Japan, where wage differentials between the automakers and their primary suppliers are small. More than outweighing any potential cost advantage of outsourcing, at least in Japan, are the burdensome logistics of packing, transporting, and unpacking bulky modules.

Note that the location of subassembly work is a separate issue from primary suppliers' still-broadening role in designing, evaluating, and guaranteeing the performance and reliability of parts. Note, too, the continuing importance of "rubbing things together" in the integral architecture of passenger cars and the related efficiencies inherent to centering the assembly work on the vehicle plants. Also note that rubbing things together is most important in manufacturing smallish passenger cars. Conducting a larger amount of preassembly away from the vehicle plants—and shortening the vehicle assembly lines more drastically—is possible and is happening in the production of trucks, specialty vehicles, and some large passenger cars.

Made-to-order production

Lean manufacturing, as epitomized by the Toyota Production System, is an extension of Henry Ford's production system. It has evolved in the direction of responding ever-more flexibly to the needs and wants of customers, but truly made-to-order production remains the exception rather than the rule. At the turn of the century, orders from end users accounted for less than half of Toyota's Japanese vehicle production.

No automaker anywhere has succeeded in accommodating individual orders efficiently and quickly in a mass-production format. Some European automakers operate plants on a largely made-to-order basis, but the lead times from order to delivery are long.

Developing truly order-based mass-production systems is a central challenge for the automobile industry in the 21st century. Addressing that challenge will require improvements in information processing, in production processes, and in supplier responsiveness to ever-changing specifications. Those improvements are likely to occur through incremental, evolutionary advances rather than through overnight breakthroughs, and they will thus depend on continuing progress in capability building.

Flexible manufacturing

Made-to-order production aside, automakers need to become more flexible in their global manufacturing. They need to accommodate a growing range of specifications in smaller production volumes and to respond better to fluctuations in demand. Building the kind of large vehicle plants common in industrialized nations will be economically unfeasible in some emerging markets. Automakers will need to achieve viability at production volumes as small as 20,000 or even 10,000 vehicles a year.

In the industrialized nations, demand will fluctuate without increasing over the long term. Automakers will need to reduce their manufacturing costs and find ways to convert some of their labor costs and other fixed costs to variable costs. Toyota has achieved somewhat variable labor costs internally with its "flexible manpower lines." As described elsewhere, Toyota deploys multiskilled workers and adjusts the range of tasks handled by each worker and the number of workers per process in accordance with fluctuations in demand. More capability building in support of that kind of flexibility will be necessary to maintain viability in industrialized-nation manufacturing.

Automated assembly

European automakers invested heavily in automating assembly work in the 1980s, and some of the Japanese automakers experimented with automated assembly around 1990. All of the automakers retreated from automation in assembly processes in the 1990s, and automated assembly is unlikely to figure significantly in competition in the automobile industry for the foreseeable future.

Vehicles are simply too big, complex, and irregular to assemble mechanically in a cost-effective manner. A dramatic shift to modular product architecture is the only conceivable development that could occasion such a shift. That could result, for example, from a dramatic breakthrough in battery-powered electric cars. But as long as integral product architecture prevails in automotive design, final assembly will remain largely the province of human handiwork.

Assisting in assembly handiwork, of course, will be a vast array of tools, including semiautomated equipment. And advances in automation will continue to raise productivity in manufacturing parts. Computerized systems, meanwhile, will increase efficiency and flexibility in automated machining centers; will support the integrated flow of work among those centers; will translate design data directly into tools and dies and, through them, into products; and will permit improved linkage between actual demand in the marketplace and production activity at vehicle plants and at parts plants. Capability building in all of those phases of automation and computerization will figure prominently in automakers' competitive standing. But human-oriented capability building will remain the chief measure of competitiveness in vehicle assembly.

Acknowledgments

The importance of capability building in the automobile industry captured the attention of the author long ago, and this book resulted from more than a decade of start-and-stop writing, frequently interrupted by the author's "day jobs." Three successive personal assistants—Toshiko Shiraki, Ai Takei, and Tomoko Iwasaki—labored hard and well on preparing the graphs and tables and on bringing order to a chaotic array of manuscripts. The author's wife, Kozue, rendered valiant service in polishing the original text. Individuals too numerous to name at Toyota, Nissan, Honda, and other companies provided insights that enriched the content immeasurably. Chapter 6, Competition, Conflict, and Cooperation, contains a great deal of material from a report written by the author while employed at Mitsubishi Research Institute.

Moriaki Tsuchiya, under whom the author studied at the University of Tokyo, instilled a positivistic outlook that has shaped the author's career. Koichi Shimokawa, of Tokai Gakuen University and Hosei University, set a sterling example with trailblazing research on the automobile industry. Yasuhiro Daisho, of Waseda University, furnished incisive guidance in regard to the technological trends summarized in chapter 8. Yukihiko Hayakawa and Kazuo Ono, at the publishing house Chuokoron-Shinsha, performed editorial magic on the author's prose. The author expresses profound gratitude to the above individuals and organizations and to all the others who contributed to this book.

Bibliography

Partial listing; only publications available in English

Clark, Kim B., and Takahiro Fujimoto. *Product Development Performance: Strategy, Organization, and Management in the World Auto Industry*. Boston: Harvard Business School Press, 1991.

Destler, I. M. (Mac). *American Trade Politics*. Washington, D.C.: Institute for International Economics, 1987.

Fujimoto, Takahiro. *The Evolution of a Manufacturing System at Toyota*. New York: Oxford University Press, 1999.

Hounshell, David. *From the American System to Mass Production, 1800–1932*. Baltimore: Johns Hopkins University Press, 1984.

Lieberman, Marvin B., and Shigeru Asaba. "Inventory Reduction and Productivity Growth: A Comparison of Japanese and U.S. Automotive Sectors," *Managerial and Decision Economics* 18, no. 2 (1997): 73–85.

Maxcy, George, and Aubrey Silberston. *The Motor Industry*. London: G. Allen and Unwin, 1959.

Penrose, Edith T. *The Theory of the Growth of the Firm*. New York: John Wiley and Oxford: Basil Blackwell, 1959.

Shimokawa, Koichi, Ulrich Juergens, and Takahiro Fujimoto. *Transforming Automobile Assembly*. Berlin and Heidelberg: Springer-Verlag, 1997.

Simon, Herbert A. *The New Science of Management Decision*. New York: Prentice Hall, 1977.

Womack, James P., Daniel Roos, and Daniel T. Jones. *The Machine That Changed the World*. New York: Rawson Associates, 1990.

Index

Page numbers in italics refer to figures.